FIRST TIME CREW

FIRST TIME CREW

Everything you ever wanted to know
but never dared ask the skipper

David Nicolle

ADLARD COLES
8 Grafton Street, London W1

Adlard Coles
William Collins Sons & Co. Ltd
8 Grafton Street, London W1X 3LA

First published in Great Britain by
Adlard Coles 1990

British Library Cataloguing in Publication Data

Nicolle, David
First time crew: everything you ever wanted to know
but never dared ask the skipper.
1. Sailing boats. Sailing. Manuals
I. Title
797.1'24

ISBN 0–229–11845–3

Printed and bound in Great Britain by
Mackays of Chatham plc, Chatham, Kent

CONTENTS

~~~~~~~

PREFACE

~~~~~~~~

Let's assume you are off on a sailing holiday for the first time. To many people such an invitation will produce both excitement and a degree of apprehension. Such a reaction is normal when one is faced with the prospect of a totally new experience. To anyone without previous knowledge of life at sea (or even simply 'afloat') the change in environment can be both stimulating and worrying.

To my mind there are two types of holiday: the luxurious and the adventurous. To some, the *QE II* appeals; to others, mountaineering. To enjoy sailing you need to be strong on the adventurous and light on luxury. Sailing, especially the deep sea variety, appeals to the romantic. As one who has been under the spell of the sea all my life I am well aware of its illogicality.

One apprehension that may exist in the reader's mind is that of actual danger, and this we can dispose of with certainty. Sailing is not a dangerous sport. The few serious accidents that do occur usually involve dinghies or alcohol or the classic combination of the two. One common fear among beginners is that of the yacht capsizing, engendered no doubt from memories of watching the strenuous efforts of dinghy racing crews to keep their boats upright. In this respect yachts are fundamentally different from dinghies. The secret lies in the word 'ballast'. All yachts have a heavily weighted or 'ballasted' keel to counteract the capsizing effect of the wind. On dinghies the ballast is the crew. Yachts are intended to sail on their sides – 'well heeled' is the term used – and it is difficult for some novices to believe that this heeling process will not continue progressively with disastrous consequences. Rest assured it will not. As the heeling angle increases, the ballast keel under the boat becomes increasingly effective and the wind's tendency to push the boat over becomes more and more reduced.

It is often said that a good cruise will have its high and low points, and somehow we need to suffer one in order to enjoy the other. True or not, I think it important to realise that it may not all be 'plain sailing'.

As for the book itself: inevitably it posed several dilemmas of which the most acute was the need from time to time to state the very obvious. When this occurs I hope the reader will be forgiving. A minor problem is the implication that the skipper will be male for which I make the excuse that it is more usual than not. It is also inevitable that some words will occur before their explanation, and I would ask that you read on regardless in the knowledge that all, eventually, will be revealed.

1

LIVING ABOARD

INTRODUCTION

The language of the sea and seafaring is one of the major obstacles that the landsman has to face when going afloat for the first time. Most will already know terms such as *cabin*, *deck* and *mast*, but you may be greeted by someone saying: 'Your berth is amidships, port side, just aft of the head.' Sailing jargon is both rich and varied and can occasionally be over-indulged in by the sailing bore, but it is surprising how much of our everyday speech is nautically derived. 'Touch and go', 'swinging the lead' and 'nipper' are survivals from that great age of sail, the nineteenth century.

Technical language is essential if skipper and crew are to communicate quickly and unambiguously. Therefore, it makes sense to attempt to learn the basics quickly as well as making your lack of knowledge clear to those in charge before you set sail.

1.1 THE BOAT

The initial impression when boarding the average yacht for the first time will be one of lack of space. Doors are narrow, decks low, bunks tiny and the galley work surfaces a joke. Prepare a three-course meal in there for six people? No way! Yet it *can* be done. I can always spot the experienced sailor when proudly showing the main cabin on my present boat. 'Isn't it lovely?' they murmur; 'Enormous amount of room,' they chorus. In fact, the actual floor area is under two square metres. The main reason for this congestion is expense: each square metre of covered deck space costs at least ten times that of a well-built house.

Boats, of course, like people, come in all shapes and sizes and it is difficult to choose one that is typical. Interestingly, boats are growing; what was considered large ten years ago is now unremarkable, a fact to which many marinas are slow to respond. Two factors are at work here: one undoubtedly is increasing affluence, and the other is the realisation that the larger the yacht the greater is her intrinsic speed and comfort. Small may be beautiful but the pocket cruiser is very much for the dedicated.

Looking at the boats available for flotilla charter in the Greek Isles, almost all are sail and average 10 to 11 metres in length. Such a boat could well be your first introduction to a sailing holiday. Aft will be the working area or *cockpit* (a word handed down from the days when live poultry were kept aboard most men-of-war). Forward of the cockpit will be a raised portion of the main deck called a *coach roof*. The deck itself will be pierced by two or three openings or *hatches*, essential in hot climates. The deck edge or *gunwale* (pronounced 'gunnel') will be protected by wires supported by *stanchions* – the *guard rail*. Forward, right in the bows of the boat, this guard rail will be totally rigid in stainless steel tubing and is known, picturesquely, as the *pulpit* (although it is more likely to be an area from which prayers or oaths are uttered rather than sermons!). A similar rigid rail may surround the stern and has been christened the *pushpit*, a pun which may become one of our less attractive nautical terms.

Being a sailing vessel, the deck area will be dominated by the mast with its supporting wires and other paraphernalia known collectively and simply as the *rig*. Indeed, all the wires and ropes are known as *rigging*; those that move (usually rope) are designated *running rigging*, and those that do not as *standing rigging*.

Below Decks

Usually access to the accommodation is directly from the forward end of the cockpit, through the main hatch and down a flight of steps or *companion way*. In many boats the cooking and navigation areas are as

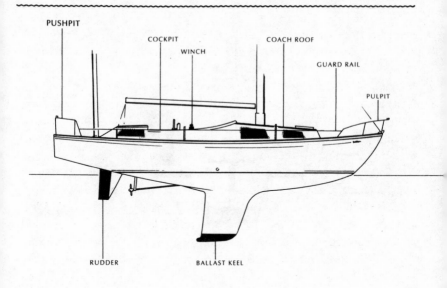

PUSHPIT

COCKPIT

WINCH

COACH ROOF

GUARD RAIL

PULPIT

RUDDER

BALLAST KEEL

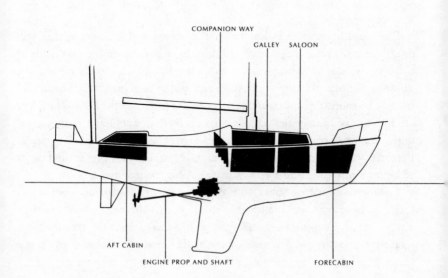

COMPANION WAY

GALLEY SALOON

AFT CABIN

ENGINE PROP AND SHAFT

FORECABIN

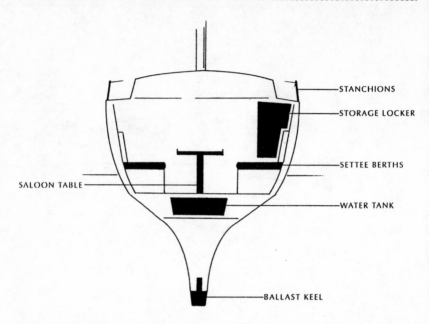

close as possible to this hatch because there are many advantages in this arrangement.

The main living area is known as the *saloon* and in most yachts will double as a sleeping area as well. An idea borrowed from the caravan is to convert the saloon table into a double bunk, the occupants having the dubious honour of being the first up and last to turn in. Other bunks will usually be found right forward and in the aft corners of the boat. The latter are known as *quarter berths*. Modern yacht designers have shown great ingenuity in creating sleeping cabins in the most unlikely places. Personally I find a more open plan preferable, trading off privacy in favour of better ventilation and a less claustrophobic environment.

Talking of claustrophobia, the ship's loo or *head* must be mentioned. Usually these are very small and in many yachts there may be more than one. The ship's plumbing arrangements receive specific treatment in section 1.8 as the head is one of the main areas of difficulty for those accustomed merely to pressing a handle or pulling the proverbial chain.

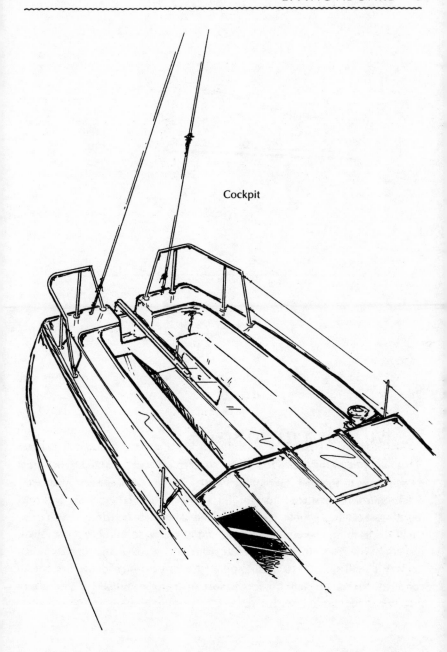

Cockpit

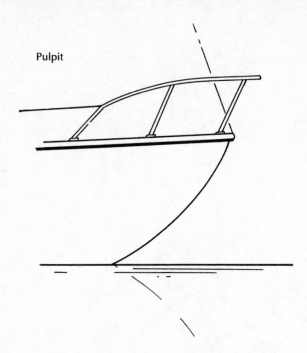

Pulpit

1.2 WILL I BE ABLE TO SLEEP?

If you are one of the lucky few who can sleep on a well padded tightrope or who have to instruct their air steward to 'Be sure to wake me when we reach Nairobi', then read no more! To us lesser mortals, getting a good night's rest can be a problem, especially if it happens to be windy. Even in a sheltered harbour there will be the sound of the wind in the rigging. I've lost count of the number of times I've turned in only to realise that there is no way I shall sleep until that tapping rope or groaning fender has been subdued. Making a yacht quiet is almost an art form and all I can do is to give you some tips and wish you luck.

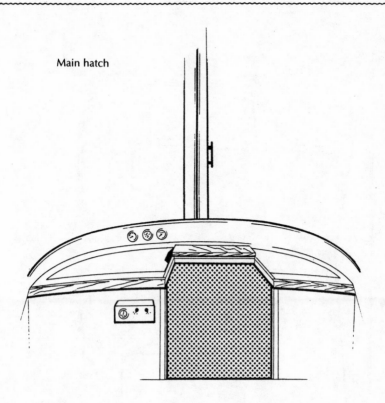

Main hatch

Halyard Tapping

Use a short cord, sail tie or shock cord to pull ropes and wires away from the mast and each other. This is called *frapping* and calls for some degree of tact or stealth if the offending noise comes from the yacht in the adjacent berth.

Groaning Fenders or Mooring Warps

Use a fifty-fifty mix of water and washing-up liquid to lubricate the appropriate point of contact. If you want to remain popular make sure you rinse the glass you use half a dozen times; few skippers appreciate detergent with their favourite whisky.

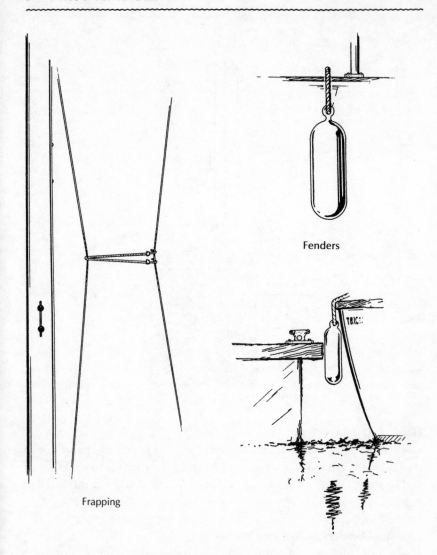

Fenders

Frapping

If you are a two-pillow sleeper bring an inflatable air cushion as most yachts provide only one. Finally, should you find your sleeping bag too restricting, unzip it and use it as a duvet.

1.3 AVOIDING SEASICKNESS

'At first you worry that you're going to die; later on you worry that you may not.' 'The only cure is to sit under an oak tree.' The jokes about seasickness, or acceleration sickness as the space medics have dubbed it, are endless.

First, let us get the problem into perspective. Each year I sail about 3,000 miles, with well over a hundred first-time sailors. Looking through my log for last year, I see that there were only three passages during which someone was ill. Before looking at the various methods which may improve resistance, a list of some of the many factors involved will be helpful.

Susceptibility
Obviously the dominant factor and one that only you can judge. However, I would point out that age plays a part here. Either we become more crafty as we become older or it really is one of the few advantages of losing one's youth.

Sea Conditions
Ridiculously obvious to mention, perhaps, but notoriously difficult to forecast. Will it be rough? This is a question I am occasionally asked and to which it is very hard to give an unequivocable reply. This is because sea conditions do not relate directly to wind strength, especially on coastal passages. Wind direction relative to the land is crucial, and tides also play a huge part in the equation. Time is important too – a fresh, new wind often produces wonderful sailing. The situation that I least enjoy occurs when sea conditions do not relate to wind strength, usually as the breeze diminishes after a prolonged blow, leaving a lumpy sea and not enough wind in the sails to steady the boat.

Size of Boat
Here I think it is true to say that for most people, the bigger, the better! A centre cockpit also helps, keeping the crew out of the ends of the boat, where the motion is worst. Remember, the Americans call it acceleration sickness.

Change of Orientation

Because the problem is very much to do with the organs of balance situated in the inner ear, the vast majority of crew fare better above deck than below. Getting up and getting dressed are common triggers.

Boredom and Fear

These are factors, and could well be the reason that children are more susceptible than adults. Always try to appear calm and confident when children are on board; in fact this is the best policy however the crew is constituted. Finding something for children to do on a long passage is difficult, especially if they can't cope with being below for very long. Letting them steer for short spells is very good, as well as posting them as look-out. If supervised, fishing with a trailing line is also very much to be recommended.

The Skipper

Yes, the skipper! After all, he is the guy who takes you to sea, decides in which direction to go and for how long. Presumably most cruises are for pleasure, so make sure that the skipper knows your views as early in the planning stages as possible. If he is a 'hell and high water' type, beware. Beware also of delivery trips and delivery skippers – they are paid by the mile and not by the day!

Body Temperature

Never allow yourself to become cold and wet. With the introduction of furling headsails, improved oilskins and spray hoods, this is now much easier to accomplish. Seasickness is much less of a problem in the tropics than in the cold waters of northern Europe.

Now for the inevitable dos and don'ts, starting with food. Almost every edible and inedible substance has been recommended by someone at some time, either as a cause or a cure-all. Here are some which, I believe, have credence:

Don't drink strong black coffee at sea; tea is much less likely to cause trouble. Ginger in any form does seem to be helpful: alcohol, most certainly, is not. (Where, I wonder, does that put Rye and Dry?) Try to create a strategy whereby you don't have to go below for the first hour or two of any long passage. Keep busy: steering is very therapeutic but initially, at least, avoid reading, navigating or cooking.

If you decide to take medication, try to get the drug into your system early. In my experience, Cinnarizine (Stugeron) has the best record with the least side effects. This drug acts on the balance organs and can be obtained as tablets or, on the Continent, as two tiny pads which are placed behind the ears allowing the drug to be absorbed through the skin.

But I have kept the best news till last: pressure pads. These are worn on each wrist and are marketed as 'Sea Bands'. At first I was very sceptical, but because they claim to have an immediate effect, I just had to try a pair. I find that they really do help. Not, of course, in every case otherwise all I'd have needed to write on this subject would be: 'Wear Sea Bands'. Instead I would say that they are well worth a try.

1.4 CLOTHING

When packing a bag for your first cruise the most important point to bear in mind is that it is just that – a bag, and *not* a suitcase. What goes into it obviously depends on the climate, which is no help at all if your intention is a summer cruise in UK waters! As someone observed, the British don't have a climate, just weather; so pack the suntan lotion along with your thermal underwear and expect everything from heatwave to blizzard. Unless you're heading for the tropics the main concern is to keep warm and dry. How you do this will depend on your pocket. At one end of the market there are firms such as Henri Lloyd and Keith Musto marketing very sophisticated sailing gear, and at the other we have Army and Navy Stores anoraks. For the first-time sailor I would advise the latter – it will be far more useful if you decide to take up golf. Sea boots are too bulky and

heavy to pack easily and I would put them well down the list. Footwear needs careful thought as the average pair of sandals or plimsolls simply will not do. Sailing shoes are generally overpriced; in fact the average marina boutique is usually unbelievably expensive. The best answer is a good pair of trainers or sports shoes – the ones with leather uppers, a cushion sole and good support for the ankle are almost ideal. They may be a little too hot at times but are amazingly tolerant of seawater. By the way, beware of sunburnt feet and stubbed toes if you elect to go barefoot.

Headgear, on the other hand, is easily acquired. A woolly hat for a cold night passage and one with a peak to shade the eyes on a hot afternoon makes sense. Like skiing, sailing can produce sun problems even when it is not especially hot so be aware of the danger of sunburn and eye-strain at sea where the light can be very intense. Today most people are sufficiently unselfconscious to dress practically rather than fashionably, but it's good for morale to have one change of clothing stowed away in which you can enjoy a meal in a smart restaurant.

1.5 STOWING AND STORING

On a well-run ship everyone should have at least one drawer or cupboard to call his own. Your bag and some items you may not need to reach regularly can usually disappear under a bunk, whilst those items that need to be hung will end up in a communal wardrobe, or *hanging locker*. Even if on board for only a couple of nights, resist the temptation to live out of your seabag. It's far better for everyone if you stow your gear away. Tidiness on a yacht is a practical necessity if things are to run smoothly. If bags are used they usually occupy bunk space and end up on the cabin floor (*sole*) at night or as soon as things get a bit rough. This will annoy some more than others, but the fact is that such clutter tends to be demoralising and can be a hazard in an emergency. When faced with what looks like being a rough trip, make sure that your personal gear is going to stay put, and that anything you may need such as gloves or oilskins is quick and easy to grab. Diving around below looking for your sea boots when the boat is well heeled and pitching will test the strongest of stomachs.

1.6 SEA COOK

Bearded Old Sea Salt: Welcome aboard. By the way, how much sailing have you done?
First Time Crew: Er, not much.
BOSS: Can you steer a compass course?
FTC: No.
BOSS: Tie a bowline?
FTC: Is that the one about rabbits coming out of holes?
BOSS: Do you know the difference between a head and halyard?
FTC: Not a clue.
BOSS: Can you cook?
FTC: Yes, I've done my share.
BOSS: Right, you're in charge of the galley.

You may only have been aboard five minutes but you now have yourself one hell of a job. Far better to have said you can make bowlines with the best of them than be responsible for a yacht's catering. Being a sea cook requires a whole range of skills, quite apart from the culinary. Dexterity, diplomacy and ingenuity are just a few that spring to mind. Offer to do your share by all means but first time at sea *and* in charge of the galley: never! Someone with several cruises under their belt would be far more suited but the trouble is that he will have the experience to have grabbed a cushy number such as navigator! Assuming the worst, if you accept the job you must get down to some hard bargaining. Take a leaf out of Old Sea Salt's book: *delegate*.

Rule 1 He that cooks does not wash up.
Rule 2 Buying supplies ashore is a shared responsibility.
Rule 3 Evening meal ashore whenever possible.
Rule 4 Breakfast is self-catering.
Rule 5 At least three minutes' notice is given to the galley slave before the vessel is tacked, gybed, stranded or sunk.

However, there is an upside to the galley business: should you make a success of it, then your future at sea is assured. As a good sea cook, doors will open, the like of which dreams are made, and your authority and standing on the vessel will rival BOSS himself.

Whether in charge of the galley or not you must make sure that you can at least make a cup of tea. In a ship's galley nowadays this means that you have to understand fully the gas supply systems. On a few older yachts you may have to master the dreaded Primus stove; on a few large ones you may have the luxury of a solid fuel cooker or an electrically heated hob, but nine yachts out of ten opt for bottled gas with its attendant risk. The danger arises from the simple fact that petroleum gases (butane or propane) have a higher density than air. If allowed to escape, gas can form an explosive mixture in the bottom of the ship. To prevent this from happening (and it must be pointed out that gas accidents on yachts are now thankfully very rare) everyone on board must understand how the gas supply is installed and operated.

The normal practice is to site the bottles in a locker outside the accommodation space with a natural drain downwards into the open air. The valve on the bottle is then kept shut unless the galley is in use. Frequently a second valve is fitted between the supply pipe and the cooker and, increasingly, a flame failure device is fitted to each gas burner. The latter is a particularly good idea because not only does it guard against gas leakage if the flame is blown out by a gust of wind but it also prevents the other most common cause of gas spillage which occurs on many yachts, especially charter boats.

The sequence of events is as follows. First someone unfamiliar with ships and galleys tries to light a burner. He twiddles the various knobs, trying unsuccessfully to ignite the gas, which is turned off at the bottle in the gas locker. Frequently one of the burners is left on. Later, perhaps with a new crew, someone else restores the gas supply intending to use the galley once various essential jobs have been done. Unless a flame failure device is fitted the gas is now free to escape. Such devices are now common and carry only the slight penalty of having to hold in the gas control knob for ten or fifteen seconds until the detector has heated up. Finally in the list of safety devices there is the gas detector, which will sound an audio alarm. Everyone on board, not just the cook, should be fully briefed on the whole system.

Still on the theme of galley safety, mention must be made of the risk of burns and, particularly, scalds. These frequently occur in port, especially at anchor when a passing vessel causes an unexpected roll. Most ship's cookers have *fiddle rails* or clamps to hold kettles and pans in position; these can make the cook's life more difficult but never be tempted to dispense with them. Take special care when working in the galley in hot climates when you may be wearing nothing but a pair of shorts or swimming gear. Under these circumstances it's a good idea to don oilskin trousers in the galley when preparing hot food under rough conditions.

Should you end up in charge of catering despite all advice, then you will also have to understand the refrigeration system and the water supply. Refrigerators and even freezers are now common aboard many yachts. The main difficulty is that they consume large amounts of precious energy from the batteries. Freezers usually run directly off a compressor driven by the engine. A half-hour run morning and evening should, with luck, keep the ship's batteries charged and the food frozen. As cook you can help to conserve electricity by opening the fridge door (or hatch) as infrequently as possible and by running the fridge cool rather than freezing. A good ploy is to turn the fridge to maximum when the engine is running and to turn it off completely at night. Water conservation is important, too, as the galley accounts for roughly half the entire water consumption of the boat.

Galley Organisation

Your first priority if day cruising should be to have stores on board that make you independent of the shore for at least two days. In this way the frustration of being unable to catch an early morning tide due to there being no bread aboard is avoided. Many countries now have semi-cooked loaves in sealed wrappers with a shelf life of several weeks. Powdered milk and a few canned meats will complete the emergency stores for use when all else fails. Storage space will be limited, so the obvious solution is to have a ready-use locker that can be replenished from time to time from various nooks and crannies that may be remote from the galley. Very often the master plan will be to find a meal ashore each evening, but it is surprising how often this intention will be frustrated, and as chief galley slave it will be down to you to produce a meal from ship's stores – so stock accordingly whenever possible.

1.7 SAFETY AT SEA

Having recently read an article in a Sunday supplement by a Professor Wolff, entitled 'Why You Should Live More Dangerously', and finding myself much in agreement with him, I would urge the reader to remember that the sea is far less of a hazard than is popularly imagined, being roughly three times less risky than driving a car (i.e. less than two deaths per billion passenger miles). Most serious accidents in yachts are drink-related and occur in port, often when using a dinghy to get back aboard after an evening meal or a boozy party on a neighbouring boat.

Safety and general safety equipment, such as life raft and radar reflectors, are the responsibility of the skipper but it is up to you as a crew member to know where your personal safety gear is stowed; by this I mean your life-jacket and possibly your sailing harness. You should also know where the fire extinguishers and the manual bilge pump are situated and how they operate. The problem that may now arise in the reader's mind is an uncertainty as to what is an acceptable level of safety equipment and what is not. Unlike cars which share a common road system, a yacht may be used to cross a stormy ocean or make a series of small day trips along a benign coastline. The best solution is, therefore, a list of safety equipment with an indication of each item's importance relative to the scope of the cruise.

Life-jackets Essential and should be the appropriate size for age and weight of user.
Safety harness Should be one or two on board every cruising yacht. One per crew member needed if the passages will be in excess of 24 hours.
Life raft Not essential unless sailing offshore, provided a good quality dinghy is carried.

Manual bilge pump

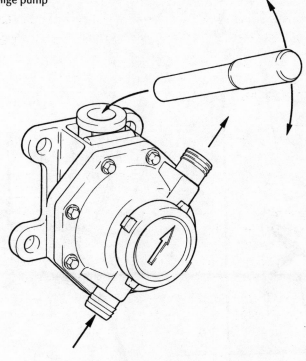

Life raft

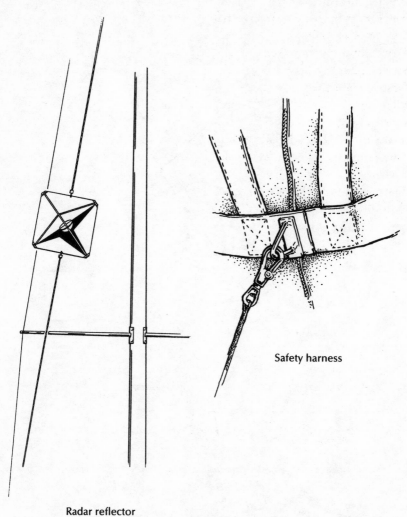

Safety harness

Radar reflector

Flares Essential. Check 'use by' date.

Radar reflector Essential for night passages and temperate climates.

Emergency steering gear Essential for wheel steering systems.

Gas detector Essential.

Fire extinguishers Essential.

Fire blanket Essential.

First-aid box Essential.

Lifebuoy Essential. One or two only. Sophisticated type needed for racing.

Engine spares Essential.

Spare anchor and long warp (rope) Essential.

Two pumping systems Essential. Could be a simple bilge pump plus a bucket.

Spare fuel and water Useful; must be securely stowed.

Two torches Essential.

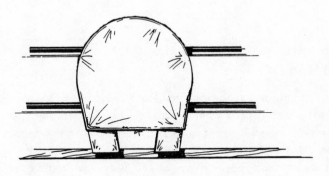

Lifebuoy

The main point to remember is that most accidents occur in harbour or anchorages, especially anchorages – you are far more likely to need a life-jacket when boarding the dinghy in a swell than when sailing in heavy airs (strong winds) at sea. Even as a new crew member you can easily find yourself responsible for a trip in a dinghy; if so, make sure you know what it is that you are taking on. Most of the present generation of inflatable dinghies are excellent craft but they are notoriously difficult to row into the wind or against the tide. If possible, use a small outboard motor but never forget to take the paddles!

Personally I've never seen anyone fall off a yacht whilst at sea but it must be the most probable danger, and for that reason Man Overboard Drill is usually rehearsed at the first opportunity. It's also a chance for the skipper to see how the crew react to the unexpected. For your part as a new crew member all you can do is to take in the drill as best you can and make a mental note that whatever happens it mustn't be for your benefit that such a manoeuvre has to be executed. To that end, when moving around the decks remember the old adage: 'One hand for the ship and one for yourself'.

1.8 THE LOO

'The loo' to be modern; 'the john' to be American; 'the toilet' to be prim or 'the head' to be nautical; whatever *it* is called, the marine version of our familiar mod con is a regular cause of difficulty to most first time crew. At home the loo is flushed without thought or effort in half a second. Unfortunately the opposite is true at sea. Why this should be so is well worth understanding. Most marine loos flush directly into the sea as it is still rare on this side of the Atlantic to fit holding tanks – on most boats there simply is no space in which such a tank could be fitted. A manually operated pump is used to draw clean seawater into the bowl and to force foul water out. The main concern of the designer is to prevent such a contraption sinking the boat. For this reason valves and anti-siphoning

loops are fitted on both inlet and outlet pipes. The latter at home may be 8 cm (4 in) in diameter, but at sea is usually 3 cm (1½ in) reducing to less than 2 cm (1 in) through the pump itself. For these reasons marine loos are very easily misused and frequently have to be 'repaired', i.e. unblocked! Because of the variety of designs, some elegant and others less so, it is impossible to advise the reader what to do, but without wishing to be too negative the opposite must be of some assistance. So here, for what it is worth, is a list of don'ts regarding marine toilets:

(1) Never use the head without first getting full instructions as to where the various valves are situated and how they must be set.

(2) Never leave foul water in the system. Remember to continue pumping after the bowl is clear so as to clear the anti-siphoning loop in the soil pipe.

(3) Never use the head as a means of disposing of bulky articles such as sanitary towels and tampons, contraceptives or even apparently harmless items such as paper towels or cotton wool.

As a charter skipper of some years' standing, I speak from the fullness of my heart – or perhaps I should say the pit of my stomach.

You may find that the strict opening and closing of valves and the need to pump the bowl dry is only necessary when at sea, and its use in port can be simplified. In this case someone has to 'see to the head' before leaving sheltered waters – a thoughtful act that can win you lots of house points. Talking of scoring points, you can win even more by remembering that many marine loos become ten times easier to pump if lubricated with a little vegetable oil occasionally (castor oil would seem to be the most appropriate!). Just pour half a cup in the bowl whenever the pump seems tight.

Finally, a word on electric razors: don't assume that there will be shaver points on board. You may have to bring the old-fashioned wet shaving tackle, or use a battery-powered shaver if the thought of using cold steel is too overwhelming.

1.9 BOAT SYSTEMS

It should by now be becoming rapidly more and more clear that modern yachts are complex; some would say that is to their detriment and that the fewer the gadgets on board the simpler and therefore more enjoyable life becomes. Not many, however, would agree. The fact is that the present trend is to recreate as far as possible all the creature comforts of a well appointed suburban house, despite the fact that a yacht is cut off from the normal water, power and communications systems. Of these three, it is power that causes by far the greatest difficulty.

There are three solutions: one is to connect the yacht whilst in port to a shore power supply. To do this both the harbour and the yacht have to be suitably equipped. The second solution is to run a generator, which is both expensive to buy and usually irritatingly noisy to run. The third and most common solution is to obtain electrical power from large car-type batteries on board and to recharge them using an alternator driven by the main engine. The weakness of this solution lies in the batteries which, despite their cost, bulk and weight, store only small amounts of energy. By running the fridge overnight or perhaps leaving a light on in the head, the boat's batteries will go flat. No problem, you may say: start the engine and recharge the system. But of course most engines are electrically started and need a healthy battery before they will spring to life. On yachts, therefore, it is usual to have a reserve battery for use only when starting the engine. As you may now appreciate, the management of a yacht's electrical power supply is a constant worry to the skipper. He needs to feel confident that the engine can be started immediately at any time, day or night, and may therefore appear to you to be unnecessarily fussy about conserving electricity.

The boat's water supply is far less critical but, depending on the size of the tanks and the ease with which they can be replenished, a degree of conservation will have to be encouraged on most cruises. It's all too common for a holiday to be dominated by having to replenish the tanks in the more ugly industrial ports rather than having the complete freedom of choice that a cruise can enjoy if water consumption is well managed. Much the same can be said of the boat's bottled gas supply. (Details of the gas system can be found in section 1.6.) The obtaining of new bottles can be very time-consuming and very costly if the bottles prove to be of a type that cannot be exchanged, and instead have to be replaced.

In these three areas – water, gas and electricity – conservation needs to be practised by everyone on board. Surprisingly there is rarely any problem over fuel, and furthermore there is little a mere crew member can do about it: the fuel system and fuel consumption are very much down to the person in charge.

But this section is about boat systems and so far we have only dealt with those which involve consumables. A list of some of the other systems on board is important as it will help the beginner to realise the complexity of a modern boat and why it is very likely that something will give trouble at some stage in a cruise.

The Steering System

This is vital and very much the responsibility of the skipper. Trouble in this area is bad news indeed, and for this reason steering systems are usually very well engineered. Rest assured; total steering failure is very rare.

The Sail System

This is known simply as the *rig*. This requires a watchful eye and usually a fair amount of minor attention. You may be able to be of help here by reporting anything that seems unusually tight or slack, frayed or loose, torn or worn.

The Propulsion System

This embraces not only the engine but also the propeller shaft, the prop itself and the stern gland. You may well have expertise in this field and this will be very welcome on any yacht. It's surprising how much time I spend as skipper of a sailing yacht working with a spanner or a screwdriver, and I am always pleased to have on board anyone with knowledge in engineering or electronics. Failing that you may have other skills such as being a good swimmer, and as such could inspect the rudder and stern gear using a diving mask. Getting the propeller clean of barnacles and weed will improve the boat's performance under power dramatically.

Tangling a rope or plastic in the propeller is all too common, and should you feel able to volunteer to clear it your popularity will be high – but don't expect it to be easy. One of the many factors to bear in mind is the risk of hypothermia even in water that seems to be at a tolerable temperature. Why such a rope must be freed and how to do it lie outside my brief but I would throw in one priceless pearl. Should the synthetic rope have melted into a glass-like mass between the propeller boss and stern tube (or '*p*' *bracket*) then one ploy that will reduce the time underwater for the diver is to unbolt the shaft from the gearbox and force it back slightly. Even a centimetre or two will allow you to get in with a hacksaw blade.

Refrigeration Systems

(See section 1.6.)

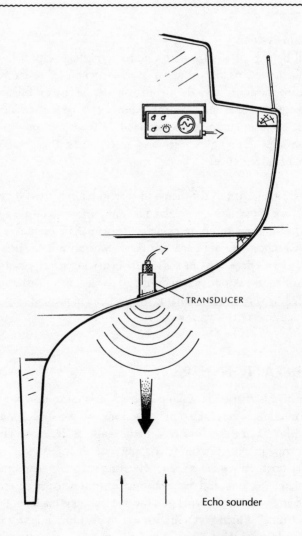

TRANSDUCER

Echo sounder

Air Conditioning System
Usually only found on yachts of 16 m (50 ft) and over. They require a generator to be run continuously and are often more trouble than they are worth.

Navigation Systems

This will be part of an elaborate electronic package especially on racing yachts. Such systems may or may not have cockpit repeaters. Should you be asked to monitor, say, the depth sounder, insist on full instructions first. Changing ranges and tuning this device are not at all straightforward. Far worse is radar. This needs expert handling from someone with no other responsibilities. Tuning the set and interpreting the display requires considerable experience.

Finally, let me return to the theme of system failure. Even if you have no expertise in the technology involved it is important to be as supportive as possible. Holding a torch, fetching tools or making enquiries ashore for expert assistance or spare parts can be of enormous help. It is also good psychology as it decreases the sense of overwhelming responsibility that is such a burden to a skipper when things go wrong. Troubleshooting, as it is now called, is very much the name of the game in present-day sailing and has, on occasions, its own rewards.

1.10 RELATIONSHIPS

The title of this chapter is 'Living Aboard' and up to now we have dealt with the nuts and bolts of the topic. Far more vital is the question of human relationships. Sailing is often a very intense experience, especially first time round. Living in close proximity, coping with the vagaries of the weather and of the boat, taking orders, and adjusting to totally new situations can be stimulating to some and demoralising for others. At sea we tend to talk of sailing and non-sailing types and the distinction is made, not on ability, but on attitude. Which you will turn out to be, only time will reveal. My advice would be to give it a try. The ability to get on with everyone on board is more important than merely having sailing skills. Given a choice between an experienced but abrasive character on the one hand and a beginner with good social skills on the other, very few skippers would hesitate to choose the latter. In the final analysis we all go to sea for enjoyment and there is a greater likelihood of the beginner becoming a useful sailor than of our experienced friend losing his rough edges.

Inevitably, the key figure on board will be the skipper and you should be very wary of spending a couple of weeks on a yacht whose skipper is an unknown quantity. Neither can you assume that, having met him ashore, you can predict his behaviour when afloat. The change that occurs to some personalities once they get behind the wheel of a yacht can be nothing less than metamorphic. Moreover, even the most placid skipper can change when racing, especially during those traumatic five minutes before the start gun. The solution, when possible, is to try a couple of day trips; failing that, talk to one of his regular crew.

Skippering styles are many and various: some of the old school demand of their crew levels of devotion to duty, determination and courage that would seldom be surpassed in time of war; others are houseproud to a degree which can only be described as obsessional. The type that always causes me most distress is the loudmouth. To him it would seem that his crew are all partially deaf or that a storm is constantly blowing. Then there is the over-cautious owner who, like the fisherman in Dylan Thomas's *Under Milkwood*, rarely if ever goes to sea at all.

One skipper, for whom I have the greatest affection, was always a great extrovert. Any passage with him was memorable: there was never a dull moment. On one trip, when butane gas escaped into the bilges, the crew was ordered to prise up the floorboards and bale the invisible gas overboard in plastic buckets. On another passage one poor guy who ate biscuits continually in an unavailing attempt to subdue his seasickness had them torn from his grasp and hurled over the side with the words, 'I'll save you the bloody trouble.'

A cruise without a crisis or two is unusual and the true connoisseur would judge it dull. The well known Sod's Law seems to operate with particular venom at sea, very often producing two or three problems simultaneously. For obvious reasons these minor crises commonly occur on charter yachts and are seldom life-threatening, although they may seem so at the time. As has often been observed, dangers at sea are usually more imagined than real.

1.11 CHILDREN AT SEA

To some parents to take children to sea at all would seem to be the height of irresponsibility, but like most situations of this type it all depends on how you set about it. In my opinion, the main danger is that the child will be put off sailing for life as a result of doing too many long passages at too early an age.

Obviously strict safety rules have to be observed for children such as not leaving the cockpit, wearing life-jackets and going below during moments of maximum activity. I have always found the best policy is to be totally honest with children. If a passage is likely to take eight hours, explain that you will start after breakfast, that lunch will be at sea and you should arrive at teatime. In this way they will not be constantly expecting the trip to end. It is this expectation that makes long passages seem interminable to youngsters. One such passage out and one back is really the most that can be asked; hopefully in between there will be plenty of short trips, sand and sunshine. The aim should therefore be to get to an area of semi-sheltered water, perhaps with a handy river estuary to explore and, with luck, a trip to an island or two.

One recipe that worked repeatedly for our young family was a canal cruise. Such a holiday is far less weather-dependent and has the important ingredient of genuine participation. At sea there is little constructive activity for a child to share in. Certainly you can keep them occupied, but they know that the running of the ship is all down to the adults and that they are merely passengers. Many yachts, once the mast is down, can make use of the European canal system; from then on the ever-changing scenery and the ability to stop almost at will are tremendous advantages. Perhaps more important is the opportunity for physical activity. A dozen locks a day is a formula that will satisfy the most boisterous of families. Most important of all is the fact that even the youngest will know that his efforts during the busy day were a significant contribution.

1.12 HOT CLIMATES

With the understandable growth in the charter business throughout the Mediterranean, especially in Greek and Turkish waters, many people experience their first cruise in high temperatures. Preparation for this is essential as fierce sunlight is more of an enemy than a friend. Many people fail to understand the devastating effect that ultra-violet light can have on their bodies. Only by gradually increasing the exposure time can serious effects be avoided. Here, then, are some tips learned as a result of sailing Caribbean waters during January and February.

(1) If possible have two or three sessions at a Solarium before travelling.
(2) Apply Factor 20 or complete blocker creams to your nose, cheeks, the top of your feet, shoulders and other sensitive areas.
(3) Use High and then Medium Factor creams on the rest of your body, even for skins less sensitive to the sun.
(4) Always cover up when sailing during the middle part of the day.
(5) Never sleep in the sun.
(6) Wear a hat.
(7) You can burn whilst swimming so wear a T-shirt in the water, especially when using a mask and snorkel.

Of course these stringent precautions only apply whilst you acclimatise, but remember that black races can also suffer from sunburn so never treat the tropical sun with anything other than respect.

Frequent showers will also be necessary to remove salt from the body after swimming, rehydrate the skin and generally freshen-up. However, make these sessions brief on board or face the inconvenience of frequent visits to ports with watering facilities. In the Caribbean this can mean joining a line and waiting your turn at the single hose available; many a valuable half day can be lost in this way.

2

HOW IT ALL WORKS

'One hand for the ship and one for yourself'

~~~~~~~~~~~~~~~~~~~~~

INTRODUCTION

In romantic literature and poetry, sailing vessels have often been compared with the beauty and grace of a soaring bird. Certainly the huge square riggers of the last century must be amongst the most wonderful of mankind's works. It may prove helpful to the beginner if we develop this analogy along more literal lines. We start, rather obviously, with a comparison of the bird's body and wings with the hull and sails of the yacht, but it becomes more interesting as we realise that in function the spars (mast, boom, spinnaker pole, etc.) are rather like the bones of a bird's wing, and the numerous ropes known as *halyards* and *sheets* are similar to sinews and tendons. The numerous winches on the boat are the equivalent of the bird's muscles. A soaring bird only puts energy into its wing muscles when some adjustment is needed via the tendons to the wing angle – a very close comparison to the crew using a winch to adjust the set of sail via a sheet. The fact that moving air and a food supply are vital to both completes the analogy.

2.1 THE RIG

This short word describes the whole wind propulsion system on a yacht. It consists of four elements:

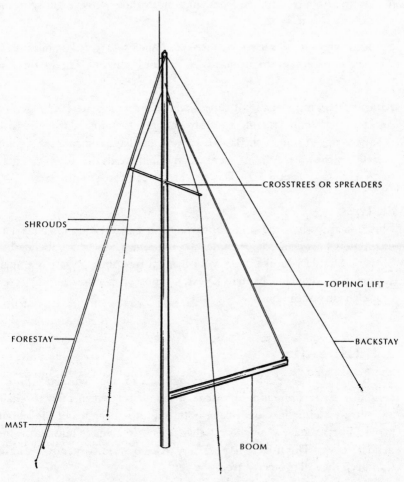

Rigging

The sails.

The spars, usually extruded from aluminium alloys, gives rigidity to the rig and support the sails.

Standing rigging This usually consists of immensely strong stainless steel wire and gives support to the mast(s). The word 'standing' implies that it is not mobile.

Running rigging Usually of rope or flexible stainless steel wire, with a rope tail, the running rigging is used by the crew to hoist and trim the sails. A square-rigged ship of the last century would have had running rigging literally by the mile. A modern crewman usually leads the running rigging to winches (see section 3.9). These are, in effect, force multipliers.

Rig Types

This is an area where the sailing bore can really get everyone yawning. The distinction between, for example, a yawl and a ketch is unbelievably obscure. Should you like to try your hand at rig-spotting there is a small section to be found in Chapter 4. Next, we must look more carefully at the four elements of the rig.

2.2 THE SAILS

Today's sails are made from strong non-rotting synthetic fibres; consequently it is rare indeed to see one fail. Their two enemies are chafe and ultra-violet light. Combatting both is a cause of much of the labour aboard boats today. One chore I always find irksome is putting on the mainsail cover. This used to be necessary to keep the sail dry; now we need it to keep the sail protected from the sun!

All modern sails are triangular. The bottom edge is called the *foot*, the leading edge the *luff*, and the trailing edge the *leach*. A *mainsail* has only one free edge, namely the leach, the foot being captive along a boom and the luff captive to the mast. *Headsails* normally have two free edges, only their leading edge being captive (to the *forestay*). The reason that

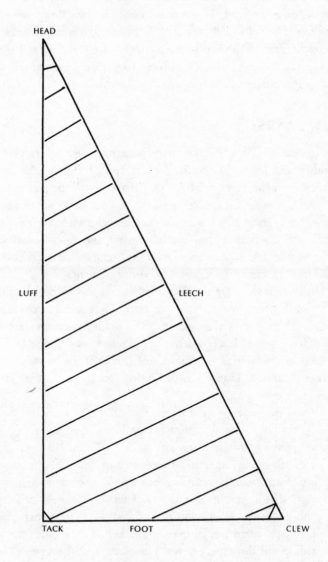

spinnakers can be so difficult to handle is their freedom of movement, having no edge fixed. They are held only at their three corners by ropes. The top of a sail logically is called the *head* and it is from this point that it is *hoisted* (raised). The top bottom corners are the *clew* and the *tack*. The clew is the corner to which the *sheets* (ropes to control the sail) are attached and is at the base of the trailing edge (leach).

2.3 SPARS

As indicated in the introductory paragraph, the spars give the rig its rigidity and form. The vertical spars are, of course, the masts. About fifteen per cent of yachts have two masts, with the smaller one usually nearer the stern. This smaller mast is known as a *mizzen* and everything to do with it is prefixed accordingly. The bigger mast has an easy and obvious label, namely *main*. Thus we have main and mizzen masts, main and mizzen sails. Incidentally, we rarely say 'mainsail'; it is always pronounced 'mainsul' or, far more commonly, simply 'the main'.

Horizontal spars are usually called *booms* and except in sailing dinghies they are kept permanently in position. They are, of course, a potential source of danger as they occasionally swing violently across the boat. 'Watch the boom' is a frequent if ambiguous cry when sailing in a breeze. Booms are only used on sails aft of (behind) the mast; only rarely is a foresail boomed. Thus on most single-masted vessels there is only one of these fearsome spars.

However, speaking of fear, mention must be made of the spinnaker. This is the large, usually colourful, ballon-shaped sail seen billowing out ahead of the yacht in so many photographs. These are not standard equipment on all boats, especially those on bare boat charter or those totally dedicated to leisurely cruising, but are of enormous help when sailing downwind in light to moderate airs. These sails have to be supported by a long boom (often called a *pole* these days) and this is usually stowed along the foredeck when not in use. Spinnaker work is both demanding and rewarding but the expertise really lies outside the scope of the first-time crew. Mention has been made because the spinnaker boom or pole, if

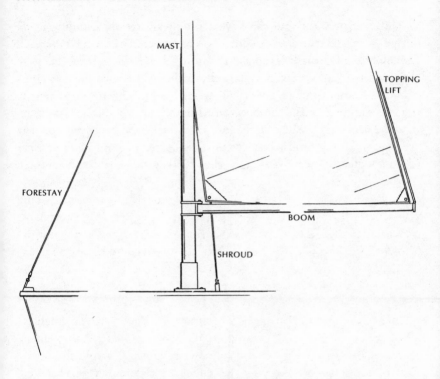

aboard, is hardly something that would go unnoticed on the deck.

Vessels of pre-war days often had more complex rigs than today's. Their wooden spars had to be shorter and to compensate were more numerous. Aboard such craft you may encounter spars with such evocative names as *gaff*, *bowsprit* and *dolphin striker*.

2.4 STANDING RIGGING

This consists of a series of wires the prime function of which is to stop the mast falling overboard. Those running longitudinally (fore and aft in sailing jargon) are called *stays*; thus we have *forestay* and *backstay*, and those supporting the mast laterally (*athwartships*) are called, rather ghoulishly, *shrouds*. To the forestay will be attached the headsail.

Unfortunately this sail can have a variety of names according to its shape, size and current fashion; *jib*, *Yankee*, *Genoa* or *genny* are all possibilities. Of these, genny is the most likely. The headsail may be attached to the forestay by metal clips called *hanks* but this system is rapidly disappearing in favour of permanent attachment. Having the yacht's sails permanently in position, with the mainsail on the mainboom and the headsail rolled up on the forestay is a tremendous advantage. The rolling or furling headsail is a comparatively recent innovation and has been adopted by many cruising yachts. This system enables the crew to

Bottle screw

rotate the forestay thus causing the foresail miraculously to appear and disappear at will. The details of the *modus operandi* will come later in section 3.6.

All the standing rigging has to be kept tight. This is achieved by means of bottle screws at the base of each wire. In some racing yachts these may be replaced by a hydraulic ram, especially on the backstay. As a novice you should never need to get involved with adjustments to the standing rigging.

There is, however, the inevitable grey area between standing and running rigging, and this concerns *runners*, or *running backstays* to give them their full title. Fortunately these are now rare and will only be found on racing yachts. Should you find yourself crewing a yacht equipped with runners take particular care to have them fully explained to you. Should you inadvertently release the runner the results to the rig could be serious. Like the mainboom *topping lift* (see section 2.5) runners should have a government health warning!

2.5 FIRST, LEARN THE ROPES

When coming aboard a yacht for the first time your first impression may well be one of ropes: ropes of differing colour and thickness, ropes hung in coils, ropes running to the shore and away into the rigging. Bewildering enough as this is, it seems all the worse because of the fact that very few ropes are ever called ropes! However, the code is logical and helpful and has to be learned, otherwise the skipper is reduced to calling at ever increasing volume, 'Pull the rope; not that rope, *that* rope; no, no, THAT rope.' Chaos.

Halyards
Ropes that hoist sails, flags, radar reflectors, etc. are called *halyards* (a corruption of haul yards). This is prefixed by the halyard's specific role; thus we have 'main halyard' meaning the rope that hoists the mainsail. Inevitably halyards are always to be found on the mast and can only be confused here with ropes which 'lift'. The latter hold things up and are normally only used to make slight adjustments. Thus we have the

mainboom topping lift, often shortened to the *topping lift*. Its job is to support the heavy mainsail boom when the sail is not in use. Be sure to find out early on if such a system is being used because to release this lift could result in the boom dropping into the cockpit with damaging results to everybody and everything!

Sheets

Very often, beginners believe that this word refers to the sails but, in fact, are ropes. However, *sheets* are invariably attached to a sail and are used to trim the sail to the wind. For this reason sheets are the ropes most in use whilst sailing. Because sails can exert very large forces, most sheets are controlled by winches (see section 3.9). The basic principles of sail trimming will be explained in section 3.1.

Guys

These ropes are usually rigged temporarily as the occasion demands and often will not be used at all. However, if the skipper is concerned about the main boom swinging across the boat unintentionally he will rig a *foreguy* or *preventer* to hold the boom permanently forward. Similarly, spinnaker booms are controlled by two guys, one leading to the bow (*foreguy*) and one towards the stern (*aft guy*). A guy that breaks all the rules because it is rigged permanently is the one holding the mainboom down; perhaps for this reason it is not called a guy but a strap, its full title being *kicking strap* or simply *kicker*. Mention will be made of its necessity later, in section 3.1.

Lines

Warps and springs, lashings and painters; this amazing collection of names is devoted to ropes that serve not the rig but the yacht herself, and their basic function is security. If, for example, the boat is lying alongside a pontoon or another vessel she will normally be held by four *warps*. The novice could be forgiven for assuming that two would suffice, one leading from the bow forward (known as a *bow line* or *headrope*) and one from the stern leading aft (*sternline*) but in addition it is usual to rig two *springs*.

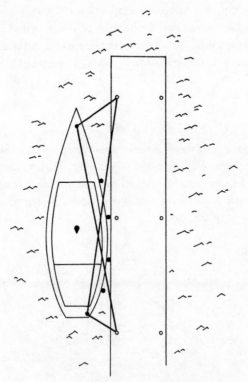

These ropes keep the boat from surging back and forth in her berth. The aft spring is attached near the stern and led forward to a point on the pontoon and the forward spring is made fast forward and led back, the two springs usually crossing each other somewhere about amidships. If conditions are boisterous, two breast ropes may also be rigged.

Painter and lashing

Two unlikely names, the latter being far less painful than it sounds and having nothing to do with the infamous cat-o'-nine-tails. The word *painter* is reserved exclusively for the rope securing a dinghy (or *tender*). When a dinghy is towed the towline is in fact the painter. *Lashings* are used to hold things down. Should it be too rough to tow the dinghy safely it will be brought aboard and lashed on to the deck or coachroof. Lashings, if they are to be tight, must be lightweight and are usually no more than thick cords. Strength is achieved through having several. Lashing down an anchor or boarding ladder is not as easy as it looks and really has to be learned at first hand under a critical eye.

Rope skills

There is, of course, no way a novice can acquire practical skills merely by reading about them. Coiling and throwing a rope, knotting and splicing, even using a cleat have to be learned first hand. All that can be achieved through the written word is to make the reader aware of these skills and when and how they are used.

Cleats

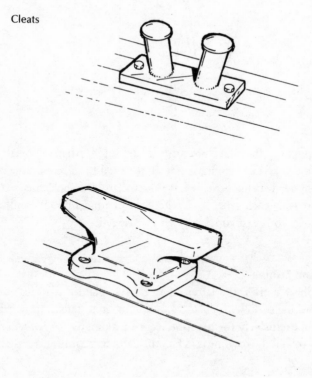

Back hitch

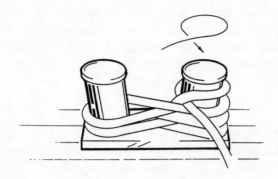

So let's start with *cleats*. The first principle of good rope management is not, strangely enough, to make sure that a rope can't come undone but that it *can* be undone (*let go*) quickly and easily. To this end we avoid knots whenever possible. The cleat can be used to hold (*secure*) a rope already under load. Moreover, a taut rope can be let go from a cleat whenever necessary. Cleats therefore have to be firmly bolted down. First, lead the rope round the base, preferably in a complete 360° circle (*turn*), and then use a figure of eight wrap-round system to build up the friction. Only after several figures of eight should a *back hitch* be put on. Personally I think back-hitching is generally overdone and can be the cause of an intractable jam on a rope if added with insufficient initial turns. A good guide to back hitches would be: sheets and guys, never; halyards, maybe; warps and painters, always. The great trick with ropes and cleats is that vital initial turn, or, in an emergency, two.

When a yacht is being berthed or moored to a buoy in a bit of a breeze the first sign of something going wrong is the skipper leaping up and down shouting, 'Take a turn, take a turn!' If you are the poor crewman on the end of a warp that clearly is about to be heavily loaded, don't stand there thinking you can hang on to it, get it round something strong (preferably a cleat or a bollard) and then hang on. This way you might just win and save the day.

At this point I can imagine many owners hurling this book overboard.

'What if . . . ?' they will say. So here are a few dos and don'ts. Don't take a turn on anything if the warp is led over instead of under a guard rail. Don't take a turn on the top of a guard rail stanchion – the base, yes, but never the top; but if humanly possible get the rope round a cleat or anchor winch a couple of times and all will be well.

Knots

It is best to know one or two really well than to have a large repertoire half learnt. I would recommend the *clove hitch* and *bowline*. Learn these well and you will be more proficient than many a skipper.

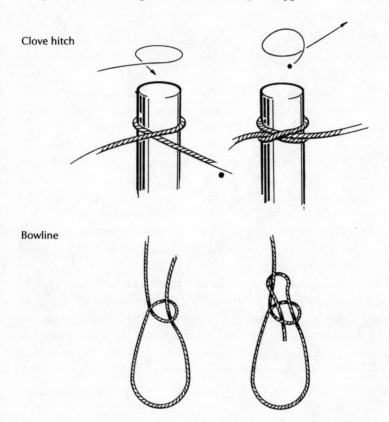

Clove hitch

Bowline

Coiling and throwing

When coiling a rope don't wrap it round your forearm. The average human forearm is too short – 'washerwoman', my father always said whenever he saw the practice. Coiling ropes is not just a question of being tidy; with care, the rope will also be ready for instant use. The diameter of the coil must relate directly to the diameter of the rope, and usually the rope itself has to be given a sharp twist with each loop – this simple skill is easily acquired with the minimum of practice.

Which brings us to the not-so-gentle art of throwing a line (*heaving* is the nautical term). Aboard large yachts, using heavy warps, special heaving lines are used but on the average yacht you should be able to throw the warp itself between three and ten metres. As with so many activities, skill and experience are more important than strength, so have a little practice session when no one is looking. Coil the line carefully with no kinks – that's the secret – and hold it in your left hand (or right, if you are left-handed). Taking about five or six coils in your right, throw with a sweeping motion, letting the coils flow out of your left hand. With the wind behind you and provided you miss your own rigging, you may surprise yourself and everyone else.

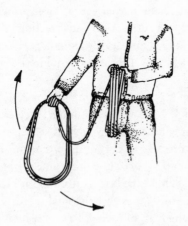

3

SAILING

~~~~~~~~~~

INTRODUCTION

A few people who sail with me regularly make no pretence of knowing how to sail; they are quite happy to pull on the sheets without knowing why. Almost like learning to fly, to some learning to sail seems mystical and unattainable. This awe of the sailing art is quite unjustified; one only has to see six- and seven-year-olds sailing confidently in their tiny Optimist dinghies to realise that it can't be that difficult. To sail really well, of course, is another matter, but mastery of the basic principles is easy. The crucial point is always to be aware of the wind direction relative to the boat. This wind angle can be judged quite easily from flags, electronic indicators or bits of wool in the rigging. Of these the wool in the rigging is the best bet.

Not surprisingly, sailing vessels cannot sail directly into the wind; roughly speaking an angle of 45° is the minimum they can achieve. When sailing at this minimum wind angle the yacht is said to be *close hauled* or *beating*. As the boat is turned away from the wind, the wind angle opens and the boat is said to be *on a reach*. If we continue turning away from the wind it begins to move behind the boat and she is said to be *running*.

Beating, reaching, running: these are the vital words to comprehend if one is to learn the fundamentals of sailing, so we must take a closer look at each.

3.1 BEATING OR SAILING CLOSE HAULED

This point of sailing is one of the most difficult and if it is your first time at the helm under sail then beating or sailing close hauled would be far from an ideal start. If the wind is from the north, let's say, then the boat can be steered approximately north-east or north-west. The 90° angle between these two courses is a no-go area. Notice the terminology, because it embraces an aberration, i.e. winds come 'from' a direction but boats and everything else (tides, etc.) go 'to' a direction.

If the skipper selects the north-east alternative the yacht will be on *port tack*, i.e. the wind will be striking the boat from the left. However, her sails will all be *set* (sheeted) on the starboard side and unless the breeze is very light, she will be leaning or *heeling* (not 'keeling') to starboard. On the port tack, the yacht's port side becomes the weather side and the starboard side

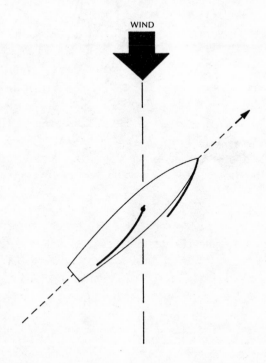

WIND

Port tack

Beating

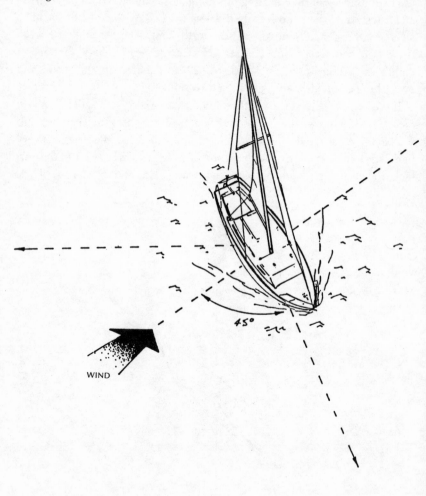

45°

WIND

can be referred to as her 'lee' side. 'Weather' and 'lee' are words in frequent use when sailing. For example, *leeway* is the boat's tendency to drift downwind, a *lee shore* is one that is downwind of the boat. When going on the foredeck, you may be advised to use the weather side of the boat. As a helmsman you may be told to 'weather that buoy', meaning to pass upwind of it. The sheets, both main and genny on a typical sloop-rigged yacht, will be in tight and the helmsman will steer so as to maintain a minimum wind angle. Too close to the wind and the sails, especially the leading edge (luff) of the headsail, will begin to stall and the boat will lose speed. Too far off the wind and all will look well but you simply will not be making the best possible progress towards your destination. How to gauge the narrow arc between these two extremes takes experience and skill. Some acquire it easily, others more laboriously.

Before leaving this topic, two more bits of jargon will be useful: 'luff up' and 'bear away'. These are the two helm orders you will be constantly given when learning to steer to windward. *Luff up* means turn towards the wind; if you are on port tack it therefore means turn to port. Do this cautiously as almost all yachts have an inbuilt tendency to turn towards the wind, especially when well heeled. (This tendency, by the way, is called 'weather helm'.) *Bear away* is the order to turn away from the wind, and in

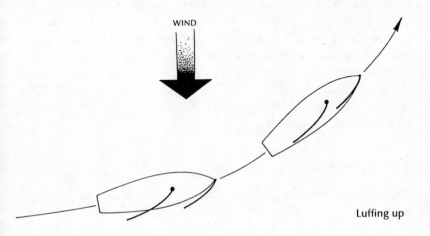

WIND

Luffing up

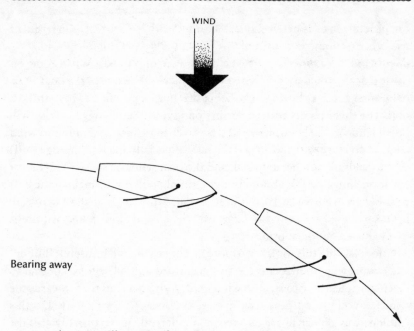

WIND

Bearing away

a strong breeze will require from you an equally strong response.

By far the best aid anyone can have, experienced or not, are lengths of wool along the leading edge of headsail. These are known as *telltales* and are usually placed in pairs either side of the sail about 30 cms from the luff. Only the bottom pair (the most easily seen) need concern you when learning the art of sailing to windward. When the wind angle is correct, both telltales will stream horizontally, indicating an undisturbed air flow. If you steer too close to the wind (too tight) the windward telltale will lift, and vice versa. Ideally you want to see the windward telltale lifting occasionally, but allowing it to lift continuously is known as *pinching*. Most beginners pinch to windward.

3.2 REACHING

This is the point of sailing that gives the best speed with minimum trouble, and it is on a reach that you should, ideally, begin your steering apprenticeship. With the wind angle nicely open of the bow at about 50° to 70° we talk of a *fine reach*; round about 90° we use the term *beam reach*. Once the wind is coming in aft of the beam, the term *broad reach* is used. As we progress from fine to beam to broad reach, the sails are progressively trimmed out: 'Ease the sheets' will be the cry – always a joyous moment after a long slog to windward with everything pinned in tight and the boat well heeled.

The novice may be surprised to learn that in light airs the fine reach is going to be the fastest point of sailing; in medium airs the highest speeds will be achieved on a beam reach. These effects are due to the speed of the vessel enhancing the apparent speed of the wind as she sails into it. Steering on any kind of reach is a joy because the wind angle is no longer so critical, and being temporarily off course is of little consequence. On a reach (unlike a beat) the wind no longer dictates the course to the helmsman. Should the wind direction alter whilst on a reach, all that has to be done is to ease the sheets if the wind shift has increased the wind angle or to tighten them in if the shift has been towards the bow. The latter is often called a 'header' whereas a wind shift aft is said to be 'freeing'. In each case

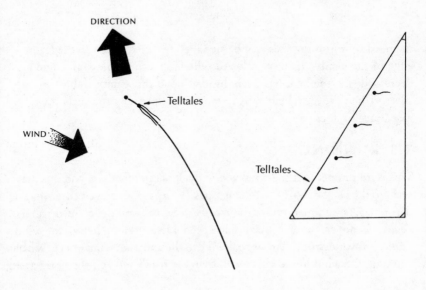

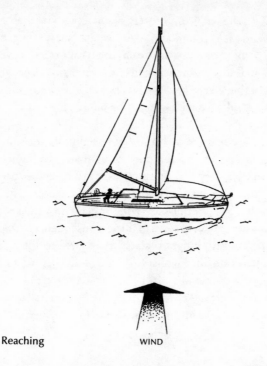

Reaching   WIND

the need to retrim the sails will be signalled by the telltales on the leading edge of the genny. If the windward telltale lifts then the wind angle has decreased (i.e. the boat has been 'headed') and this entails tightening the sheet. When the lee telltale fails to stream horizontally the sheet must be eased until it does.

3.3 RUNNING

This term implies that the wind is now well behind the boat and this may seem to the beginner to be excellent news. There are, however, three snags: these may be summed up by the words *slow*, *roll* and *gybe*. Surprisingly yachts do not sail at their maximum speed when running before the wind unless it is very strong. This is again due to the apparent wind effect. When running, the wind in the sails is less than the true wind and the faster you sail the less strong the wind becomes. The answer is to increase the yacht's sail area and this is precisely the role of the spinnaker.

Next, rolling: the only time a sailing vessel will roll appreciably is when running and this can make steering difficult. There is a definite rhythm and feel to the helm of a yacht running before the wind, and an experienced helmsman will anticipate the boat's tendency to swing off course. Steering before the wind in moderate or rough conditions keeps the helmsman busy but there is at least one bonus: the decks stay dry and there is a degree of exhilaration. However there is, especially on a dead run (wind dead astern), the constant worry of an accidental *gybe*. This rather strange word describes a manoeuvre in which the wind moves across the yacht's stern. When the manoeuvre is planned all is well, but an involuntary gybe due to inexperienced helming puts an enormous shockload on the rig and is of great danger to the crew as the mainsail boom swings uncontrolled across the boat through an arc approaching 180°. (A controlled gybe will be described later.)

Running   WIND

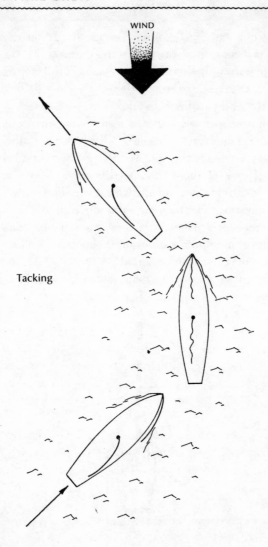

WIND

Tacking

3.4 TACKING

Tacking is the most routine of all sailing manoeuvres. Basically it is the method by which a sailing vessel works her way up into the wind. Let's imagine that your sloop-rigged yacht is attempting to sail northwards against a northerly wind; as has already been seen, the choice of headings will be either north-easterly or north-westerly. Suppose the north-westerly tack is chosen, then the genny will be pulled in tight (*sheeted*) on the port side of the boat and the yacht will be heeling to port. (Note, however, that you are on a *starboard tack*.) After making progress in this north-westerly direction for some time, the skipper will want to change tacks and head to the north-east. This change of tack is called *going about* (or *tacking*). On most boats the routine will be as follows: the call will first be 'Stand by to go about' or 'Ready about' followed by 'Lee ho'.

The helmsman usually takes charge of the manoeuvre and the first order is intended to warn the crew to prepare. Normally the mainsail will look after itself during a tack and the crew only have to deal with the headsail(s) and possibly the runners if the boat has them (see section 2 .4). On the leeside of the cockpit (this will be the portside if you are on starboard tack) one crew member will take the sheet off its cleat or off the self-tailing groove on top of the winch and hang on to it. On the weatherside (the high side if heeled) another of the cockpit crew will have found the 'lazy' (unused) sheet and will have made two turns around the winch (always clockwise) in readiness for the manoeuvre. Once this is done the helmsman will give the executive command 'Lee ho' and will turn the boat smartly into the wind. The crew holding the sheet will throw the turns off the winch as soon as the boat starts to come more upright. Their job from now on is to make sure that the sheet continues to run out freely. 'Don't let the sheet foul' may well be the instruction you will receive. On the other side the slack in the lazy sheet must be rapidly gathered in. Fast work now will save much labour on the winch handle. As the sail begins to fill on the new tack, the load on the sheet (no longer lazy) will increase rapidly. The crew will whip two more turns on the winch (making four in total), the winch handle will be inserted in the top of the winch, and the long wind begins until the sail is adequately sheeted – usually when it is just touching the lee shrouds. Handling the winches on a yacht is a skill that will be described later (see section 3.9).

Should you be given the helm for a tack, the most important priority to get fixed in your mind is the new direction the boat must take on the opposite tack. This will always be roughly at right angles to your present course (remember the minimum 45° angle to the wind on each side). If possible, find something to aim at before you go round (a chimney on the land or a distant buoy), as you may find the whole manoeuvre disorienting at first.

3.5 THE GYBE

In many ways *gybing* the boat is the opposite to tacking. It entails putting the stern through the 'eye' of the wind instead of the bow, and the cockpit crew's main preoccupation is with the mainsail rather than the genny. Gybing in a breeze when under spinnaker is the ultimate manoeuvre and detailed instructions would run for many pages. Gybing occurs far less frequently than tacking, and the skipper can always opt out of a gybe by going the long way round and tacking instead – few do.

First, let's set the scene. Typically, a gybe will occur when rounding a buoy or a headland. The boat may be steering north, running before a good breeze from the south-south-west. (Note that with the wind coming over her port side she is on port 'tack' even though she is running.) Her mainsail will be well freed off way out over her starboard side. It may be guyed forward (see section 2.5) to stop the boom crashing over accidentally if the seas are breaking. The genny will be doing little for the boat unless it has been put out on the port side on the end of a pole or spinnaker boom.

A gybe will arise if the course has to be altered to the east, i.e. to starboard, because this will bring the wind in over the starboard side of the boat, necessitating a change in the setting of the sails. The order 'Stand by to gybe' should produce a flurry of activity from the crew. First, the pole will have to be got down if it is in use on the genny, and the foreguy on the mainsail boom removed. This will entail work on the foredeck and a prudent precaution would be to use safety harnesses. Having cleared this encumbrance the main sheet will be brought in. The genny can be ignored if the boat is short-handed (short of crew) or rolled up out of the way if furling gear is fitted.

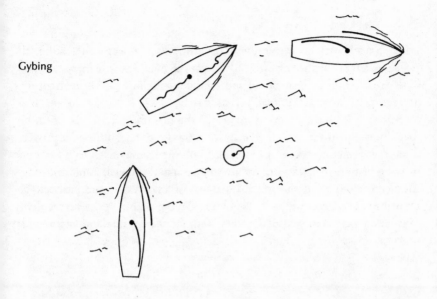

Gybing

WIND

The executive command is 'Gybe oh' and the helsman alters course to starboard away from the wind. Usually the mainsail hangs fire for a dramatic second or two before whipping across the boat. A good crew will let the mainsheet surge round the mainsheet winch (or round a cleat on a smaller boat) rather than stop the sail dead. However it is done, there will be quite a bang as the boom whips over. Remember to keep yourself clear of the boom and the mainsheet as this happens. With the yacht settled on her easterly heading the main can be trimmed and guyed if necessary and the genny can be set on the port side. Of course, your first gybe may well be in light conditions, in which case you may be hardly aware of it. Such is the contrast between light air sailing and, say, a good breeze of 20 knots (Force 5).

3.6 SAILS UP, SAILS DOWN

Having dealt with tacking and gybing, running, reaching and beating, all we have left is getting the sails on and off the boat. (Surprisingly 'on' and 'off' are the normal terms used and include reducing sail, i.e. reefing.)

Hoisting sail, or making sail as it used to be called, is easily accomplished nowadays. With the mainsail cover off, the main halyard attached to the head of the mainsail, and the yacht heading out of harbour under power, the crew remove most of the sail ties holding the mainsail to its boom, leaving just one or two until the order 'Up main' is given. With the yacht head (bow) to wind the sail is hoisted, usually by a direct pull on the halyard, and then tensioned on a winch. On big yachts the halyard will be wire and will be winched all the way. With the sail up and flapping the crew

Furling gear

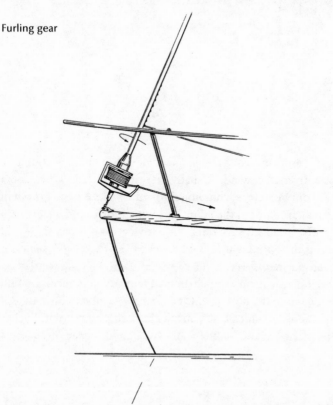

may have to adjust the kicker, the tension in the foot of the mainsail and topping lift (see section 2.5) depending on how sophisticated the mainsail is. Note that on many yachts the main halyard is led to the cockpit and hoisting the mainsail is carried out from there rather than from the mast.

To *drop* the main the procedure is reversed. Having the boat's head into the wind is now less critical. The crew make sure that the topping lift is correctly trimmed to prevent the boom dropping onto heads in the cockpit, and then simply release the main halyard, assisting gravity to bring the sail down. It is important for everyone available to help to get the sail rolled up and on to the top of the boom out of the way of the helmsman. Until this is done the view forward from the cockpit is severely restricted. Plenty of sail ties need to be handy. Despite their name it is best not to tie these but simply to pull them tight and twist the ends under three or four times; if a canvas sail tie is knotted tightly and subsequently gets wet it is a devil to undo.

Now for the headsail(s). Statistically the most likely method will be by means of furling gear. This system leaves the sail permanently hoisted and rolled up (*furled*) around the forestay. To *set* such a sail is simplicity itself. The yacht will normally be sailing under main, perhaps on some sort of a reach; when the genny is required the furling rope is released and the sail is unrolled by pulling on the appropriate (*lee*) sheet. Don't be tempted to pull on the sheet directly; as the sail rapidly unrolls, its full power will be unleashed and you must have a winch between you and the sail. Two turns once again is about optimum, plus two more before the handle is brought into action.

The jib furling rope usually runs from the cockpit through a number of small blocks at the base of the guard rail stanchions to a large drum at the base of the forestay. When the headsail is no longer required the crew will release the sheet, the sail will *flog* (flap), but with the crew pulling lustily on the furling rope the drum will rotate and the sail will rapidly become a docile roll of fabric on the forestay. In a strong breeze a winch may be needed on the furling rope; in a light breeze the crew will have to apply light resistance to the sheet in order to induce a neater, tighter furl in the sail.

Hoisting conventionally rigged headsails (i.e. non-furling ones) starts with a decision as to what size sail to hoist. Start by attaching the *tack* of the sail to the base of the forestay. The tack can always be identified by the sailmaker's logo which will be in this corner of sail. The leading edge of the sail (luff) is then attached to the forestay by a series of spring loaded clips called *piston hanks*. Care must be taken to clip these on so that they are all 'looking the same way'. By cross hanking, many a forestay wire has been ruined. With much flogging about, the sail is hoisted and tensioned by a winch, and finally sheeted in – peace.

To lower such a sail follows an easy and predictable pattern, but unlike a furling sail it severely restricts any foredeck activity until it is unhanked and bagged.

Hoisting, setting and dropping spinnakers in one piece is once again a little too complicated to describe from a novice's point of view. Suffice to say a great deal of ingenuity has been expended in devising methods of hoisting these powerful sails without them filling with air. A series of expendable rubber bands or a huge sock that engulfs the sail are two of the better ideas.

3.7 REEFING

Getting sail off the boat can also mean reducing sail area (due to an increase in wind strength) and is generally referred to as *reefing*. As a first time crew there is no way you should find yourself responsible for this activity, but in order to assist someone else intelligently, an outline of what may be involved is worthwhile.

All mainsails are capable of being reefed, and the most common method is termed *slab reefing*. What has to be accomplished is the reduction of the lower portion of the sail in one, two or three increments – first, second and third reef. Generally the pressure of wind in the sail is reduced by easing the mainsheet and kicker. The main is lowered until the appropriate reefing *cringle* (a metal ring in the luff of the sail) can be engaged into a strong hook on the boom. The halyard is then retensioned. The trailing edge of the sail (leach) is now pulled down on a reefing line via the inevitable winch, and

Reefing mainsail

the reef or slab is 'in'. The loose bag of sail now flapping about below the boom is tidied up with a reefing line that is threaded through special holes in the sail and under the boom. The now much less common method called *roller reefing* rotates the boom and accomplishes the same effect of reducing the lower portion of the sail.

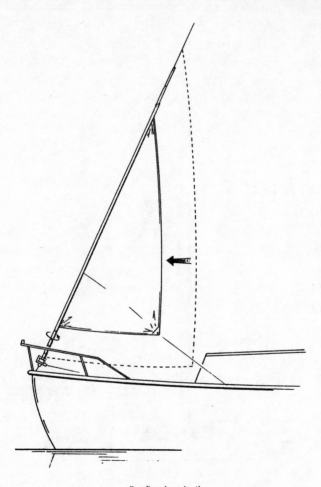

Reefing headsail

There are also two distinct methods of reefing headsails; this time the most common is a rolling method. On a furling headsail all that has to be done is roll up into the furling gear whatever percentage of sail is not required. The best method is to let the sheet fly and, as smartly as possible, roll the sail up completely. Then one crew member moves the sheet lead forward and a reduced sail is reset by cautiously easing the furling line as someone winches in on the sheet until a sufficient area of sail is re-exposed to the wind. Such a reef does not produce a particularly efficient sail shape but the alternative is quite a challenge! This entails taking the entire headsail down and substituting a smaller one, which is exactly what is required in yachts without furling gear. A headsail change under rough conditions will daunt all but the toughest crews, and this fact alone explains the present popularity of furling gear.

3.8 STEERING

Inevitably quite a lot has already been covered on steering but a few very basic ideas will not be amiss, assuming that the reader is truly a novice. First off it must be pointed out that there are two totally different steering systems in use. On small to medium-sized boats it is quite usual for there to be nothing more than a long lever called a *tiller* acting directly on to the upper part (stock) of the rudder. The alternative, of course, is to have wheel

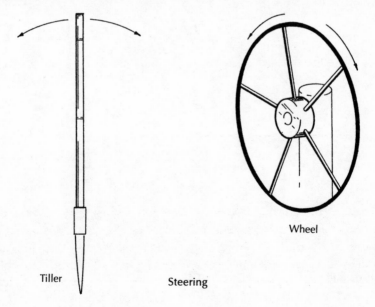

Tiller   Wheel

Steering

steering. In this case the rudder is controlled via wires or shafts by a wheel in the cockpit. The current passion is to use truly enormous wheels, their size being partly due to the need to achieve the necessary degree of leverage and partly, I suspect, because they look impressive. But the implication is clear; there will be occasions when steering requires both hands and a good deal of strength.

The fundamental difference between wheel and tiller steering, from the helmsman's viewpoint, is that they act in exactly opposite ways. When steering with a wheel a turn to port is achieved with an anti-clockwise turn of the wheel to port, whereas a tiller arm must be pulled to starboard to achieve the same effect. The fact that all outboard motors steer the dinghy tiller-style makes life difficult for the beginner if crewing a yacht with wheel steering.

The most common difficulty aboard my boat arises from having someone at the wheel whose previous, if limited, experience has been with tiller steering. They suffer from what has been christened 'tilleritus' – a syndrome of occasionally turning the wheel the wrong way. Usually there

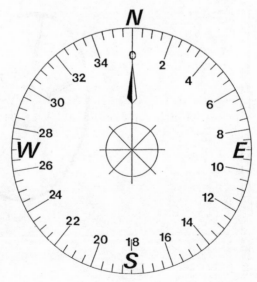

Compass card

is a chorus of advice to steer 'like a car', and it is interesting and informative to analyse the difference. Certainly, like cars, yachts turn right when the wheel is turned clockwise but there the similarity ends. A car always responds positively whereas a boat in a seaway will not. Moving the wheel a given amount produces a varying response, and it is this that can cause a crisis in the helmsman's mind. The other basic difference lies in the way in which you control a turn once it is initiated. At sea the wheel must be gradually *centred* ('eased' is the old term) in order to control the turn and stop the swing on the desired heading. Certainly, with the virtual disappearance of the long straight keel of older yachts, modern yachts are much harder to control in breaking seas than their predecessors.

Undoubtedly the best introduction to steering is under power in uncongested waters that might be described as being smooth or slight. At the other end of the scale would be steering a compass course in a heavy following sea. Compass steering is harder than it looks because the human eye misleads the brain into believing that the compass card is gyrating around relative to the boat, when in fact it is the card that is stationary (hopefully it will be locked on to the magnetic pole) and it is the boat that is moving. The reference line called the *lubber line* must be kept adjacent to the required heading.

'Steer zero four five' might be the order. This is 45° to the right of due north, i.e. north-east. Usually the compass card is only numbered every 20°, and only every 5° is marked with a line. Moreover 20° (or zero two zero) would be simply the figure 2 on the card (if you see the figure 20 it denotes 200°). Suppose the lubber line reading is '4' (i.e. 040°) then you need to turn the boat gently to the right to get 045°. 'Lubber line to the reading' is the golden rule. Remember you have control of the lubber line, not the compass card.

3.9 WINCHES

Because the sails can produce very large loads, all yachts have simple machines or force multipliers to aid the crew. In the past this was usually a pulley system (known as a block and tackle at sea) and this is still used to

Winch

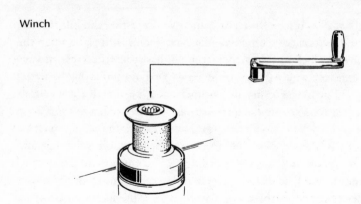

control the boom on most yachts and dinghies. Now, however, it is very much the age of the winch. There may be a dozen or more on a large racing yacht and the bigger versions, giving a force multiplication of, say, sixty-five, cost a fortune. Despite their cost and sophistication, they are not powered. You supply the energy through nothing more complicated than a handle. Even the anchor is still raised by hand on most sailing vessels, especially those under 40ft in length.

The biggest winches, known as the primaries, are found on either side of the cockpit and their job is to help you deal with the very considerable forces exerted by the yacht's headsail (genoa/jib/genny, etc). This sail may be dragging the yacht along faster than her engine so remember that there can be an awful lot of horse power on a genoa sheet in a good breeze. For this reason, your first attempts to get to grips with a powerful sheet winch should be in port or in a light wind.

Let's suppose the helmsman wants the sheet tightened; he or she will probably say something like: 'In on the genny sheet.' First, remember to head for the leeside of the cockpit (on the weather side will be the unused or lazy sheet). Next find the winch handle – usually kept handy but not in position – and place it into the top of the winch. If it won't go in, deal with the safety lock mechanism. Provided the winch is of the self-tailing variety, all that has to be done is to wind. But let's be quite clear about this: sailing is a very physical sport. One of its many appeals is that you can really let rip with all the strength you can muster, technique and determination playing just as important a role as brawn. If the sail is really pulling, you simply cannot expect to manage sitting down. In fact, it is best to straddle the cockpit coaming (edge) so that your breastbone is directly over the winch centre. In this way you can use your shoulder muscles and bodyweight to full advantage. Wear a safety harness if conditions are at all rough. The direction in which you turn the handle depends entirely on the winch design and its gearing. One obvious ploy is to try both directions and see which one is the easier. By the way, don't worry about the sheet going out instead of in as winch drums are designed never to turn anti-clockwise.

Non self-tailing winches really need two crew except in light airs. As a beginner you may be asked to do the tailing. This simply means that you have to exert a firm, steady pull on the sheet to create the friction that will bind the rope to the winch drum. Never let go! When the crewman ceases winding, keep a steady pressure on the rope, lead it to a cleat and make fast.

Now for going the other way – letting the sheet out. This, of course, is all

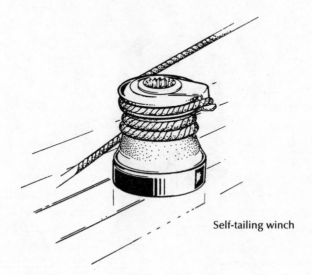

Self-tailing winch

technique and good co-ordination. Take the sheet off the cleat or out of the self-tailer, keeping a steady, positive pressure on the rope at all times. Next reduce the number of turns (360° twists) on the drum to three. Be careful to maintain the pressure. Now carefully decrease your pull on the sheet and it will surge round the winch but under your control. To improve control and to prevent what are called riding turns, try placing your free hand on the winch drum and exerting pressure on the sheet to increase friction control.

Tacking

The loaded lee sheet must be stripped off the drum smartly but *after* the boat begins to turn. This greatly reduces the shock to the rig which occurs if the sheet is let go prematurely. If sufficient crew are available, make it your job to see that the whole length of the sheet is allowed to run out freely. On the other winch, the crew should have two clockwise turns already on the drum. As the yacht tacks they will take in the slack as rapidly as possible, pausing only briefly to whip on the third and fourth turns as the load increases. One then winches, using the higher gears first on the more complex winches.

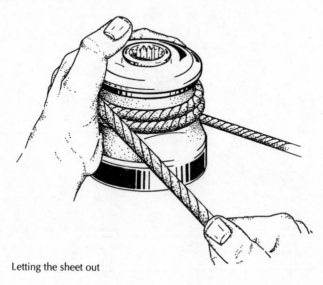

Letting the sheet out

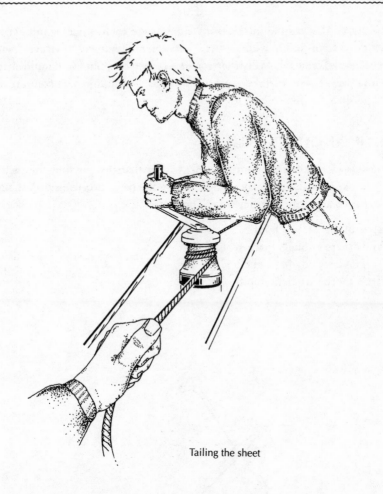

Tailing the sheet

Finally, three rules about turns round winches:

(1) Always clockwise, no matter which side of the cockpit you are. If in doubt, say when using a mast winch, spin the drum first; the direction in which it is willing to go is the one to follow.

(2) Always keep a winch and at least two turns between you and any sail.

(3) Don't imagine that it would be easier to put on all the turns right from the start. This results in the turns riding over each other, jamming the whole system solid. Riding turns occur from time to time even with experienced crews. Usually they can be winched out, but you should check with a senior crew member before doing so. A misjudgement could result in the sheet having to be cut.

3.10 ANCHORING

There is a lot more to anchoring a yacht safely than just pitching the anchor or 'hook' over the side. By understanding the basic problems you should be able to assist more efficiently. These are:

(a) Will the anchor hold?
(b) Is there enough space around us?
(c) Have we adequate shelter?
(d) Is there sufficient depth of water?

Fisherman's anchor

CQR anchor

Bruce anchor

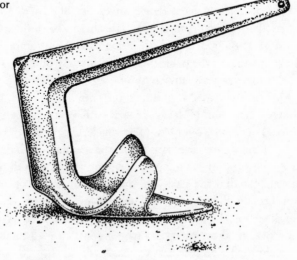

The question of the anchor gripping the bottom, or *holding* as it is termed, is largely a matter of a good quality anchor of sufficient weight plus enough chain or rope to get as horizontal a pull on the 'hook' as possible. The quality of the sea-bed is vital and terms like 'good holding' or 'poor holding ground' are used in the detailed sailor guides or *pilots*, as these books are called.

Enough space for the yacht to swing clear of other vessels and obstructions is another difficulty that deters skippers from anchoring. It is often hard to predict where the boat will actually end up, as the distance the anchor has to be dragged before it buries can vary enormously. A change of tide or wind direction will alter the whole geometry of an anchorage. The accepted rule is that the last vessel to anchor must move if it is found that two boats look as if they will touch. Quite often it takes more than one attempt to achieve a satisfactory position.

The question of adequate shelter is vital, especially if an undisturbed night's sleep is high on the agenda. Again a change in the direction of the tide or wind will transform a tranquil anchorage to a rolling nightmare. The depth of water is rarely a problem in the tideless cruising areas of the Eastern Mediterranean or the Baltic; however, in the Channel Islands, for example, tides frequently have ranges in excess of 10m (33ft) and the calculation predicting the depth at low water has to be understood.

All this information may be of little immediate use to the beginner, but an awareness of some of the problems can ultimately only be of benefit.

Now for some practical advice about letting anchors go and their recovery. On small yachts this will be done entirely by hand, but once a vessel is longer than 10m (33ft) it is usual to have a manually operated anchor winch. If a vessel is over 13m (43ft) an electrically powered winch is often fitted. Of these three alternatives it is the manual winch that calls for most skill as well as good staying power when the 'hook' is down in deep water. Like almost all foredeck work, dropping the anchor benefits from preparation. Usually the anchor has to be unlashed, a handle found and the clutch or brake released. Provided you are in calm waters, it is a good idea to get the hook over the bow roller and hanging just clear of the bow wave. When the anchor is let go it is best to release the anchor chain in two or three bursts rather than all at once. This will stretch the cable out over the sea-bed and keep it clear of the anchor itself. The cable should be marked in lengths (there is no standardised code as yet) and the skipper will indicate how much chain he wants out (*veered* is the traditional word). When the brake is applied the cable should go tight, bringing the boat to an abrupt halt; failing this the anchor may have to be driven home by coming astern on the engine. If anchoring near rock or in an area of old permanent moorings a trip line may be attached to the crown of the anchor before it is released. Generally speaking trip lines are a nuisance and often cause more trouble than they save.

To get an anchor up, especially if the skipper is determined to sail off without help from the engine, requires a good deal of muscle. Usually much help can be given to the foredeck crew by using the engine. On larger yachts a useful role for the beginner is to stand amidships and relay information from the foredeck to the cockpit. This is a matter of directing the helmsman to steer up the anchor cable at the correct speed. If the anchor is well buried after a bit of a blow, the forward momentum of the boat can be used to break the anchor out of the sea-bed. Again this requires good co-ordination between the two ends of the boat.

3.11 ROUGH SEAS

For an experienced crewman, coping with rough weather is all part of the sport; for the beginner, rough water will seem very intimidating. On a broad reach or on a run, big seas can be great fun, progress is fast and the decks stay dry except for the odd splash. It's when sailing into the wind that rough seas become hell – that is for 99% of the human race. Progress under sail is painfully slow and, for every two or three yards gained, one is rewarded with a bucketful of salt water right between the eyes (and usually down the neck).

Most novices are fearful for the vessel herself: 'Is she seaworthy?' they ask. The fact is that up to storm conditions almost all vessels will manage to stay afloat, but with varying degrees of disarray. There is an increasing risk to the rig as the wind rises but undoubtedly on most yachts the weakest link will be the crew.

If you should find yourself involved in a discussion as to whether or not to sail I would always advocate going to have a look and putting back into port smartly should things be really nasty. Ideally, your first encounter with, say, Force 6 plus should be on a short downwind passage.

As a junior member of the crew one of the most helpful jobs you can take on, and one that is often neglected, is to prepare the boat below decks for her impending encounter with rough water. Check that the forward hatch is latched tight, that the heads are pumped dry and all ventilators screwed down. Next, do what we call a 'rough water stow' of all loose gear. Knowing which way the boat is most likely to be heeling is essential. As you proceed to sea and before you reach open water make sure your safety harness is on correctly and comfortably and that you have done all you can to ensure you stay dry. A small towel worn as a scarf is very useful to catch stray drips. If you have galley responsibilities make sure that what you plan to eat and drink is to hand but secure. Check all doors, both large and small, are closed or latched open. Finally, and perhaps by this stage belatedly, review your precautions against seasickness (see section 1.3).

3.12 NIGHT PASSAGES

Almost all night passages are memorable, sometimes for the right reasons and sometimes not. Experiences at sea at night are heightened if, for example, the yacht is slipping along nicely and it feels as if she is going like a train; if conditions are a little rough then the seas seem enormous. Every action is also that little bit more difficult to carry out at night and what would be a minor problem in daylight can be a major one in the dark. Judging distances becomes very much harder and it needs an experienced watchkeeper to keep a sailing vessel on a safe path at night in a shipping lane or near a fishing fleet. As a beginner your main preoccupation will be in keeping warm as it is seldom anything other than bitterly cold on most night passages, even in the summer.

So what will you be doing during your three- or four-hour stint on watch? Well, first and foremost the latter – keeping a good look-out or watch, maybe a bit of steering, teamaking, sail trimming and perhaps, if you're lucky, some star gazing. Should the watch leader leave you in charge for half an hour or so, rule number one is not to leave the cockpit under any circumstances. The most common mistake is to delay calling the watch leader for too long when faced with a rising wind or a close encounter with some mighty supertanker. If the yacht is being steered by her autopilot make sure you know how to disengage it so as to obtain manual control of the rudder in an emergency – the most common of which will be avoiding unlit fishing gear.

3.13 GETTING ASHORE

Before we start on the dinghy instruction a word about the etiquette of crossing other boats when moored two or more abreast (*rafted up* is the term that is now in vogue). To minimise the intrusion it is customary to get ashore by crossing the neighbouring yachts via their foredecks rather than the cockpit area. If the owners are on deck, first ask permission to cross their boat, and then do so with a light foot.

Now for some detailed dinghy advice as the few statistics available clearly indicate that using the dinghy is when most yachting accidents occur. Typically, the dinghy will be an inflatable craft and it is more likely to be propelled by a small two-stroke outboard than a pair of oars. The new generation of outboard motors is far more reliable than its predecessors and in many ways makes life not only easier but safer. A dinghy powered by oars not only has less room to manoeuvre but is far more vulnerable to adverse winds and tides. Many of the tiny outboard engines weigh only 10kg or so and are therefore easy to lift on and off. Nonetheless, I would recommend the use of a safety line, especially for the bigger engines.

For a short journey all you need are the oars (or paddles, as they are often called). For use at night or in open water you need, in addition: petrol can,

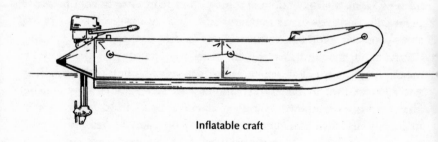

Inflatable craft

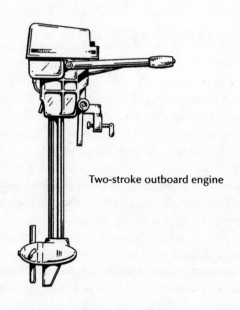

Two-stroke outboard engine

bellows, flares, torch, engine spares and perhaps a light anchor. I personally don't advocate the automatic wearing of life-jackets but for some people and some journeys they would be very appropriate.

Getting in and out of the dinghy can present a problem, especially on modern yachts with their high topsides. The very lightness of the dinghy is also a hazard as it will slip away from under you if you try any dramatic leaps for terra firma. So, point number one is to hold the dinghy firmly to the ship's side whilst people get in or out. It's best to do this amidships as the yacht will pitch less there than at the stern if there is an unexpected wash from a passing ferry.

Getting on to a beach in a bit of surf is a real picnic. If you are in charge be prepared to call off the attempt if the waves are more than a half metre or so. It must be clearly understood that at least one person will have to get his or her feet wet so settle who that's going to be well in advance. In light surf it's best to come in stern first under oars. Don't forget to switch off the petrol supply to the engine at least a few seconds before stopping the motor and raising the engine to avoid damaging the propeller on the beach.

Getting off a beach in surf is difficult – and impossible to accomplish without most of the crew getting well splashed. The basic plan is to watch the waves for some time in order to establish (a) where there is least surf and (b) the sequence of large breakers followed by smaller ones. Once a decision is reached as to when and where to launch, the idea to instil in everyone is the need to move fast and decisively. Getting out of a dinghy is a great way of learning some of the laws of physics – the hard way. Unless you are both an athlete and an optimist never try leaping ashore from any lightweight craft. Even if you succeed your fellow occupants will not share in your brief moment of glory – they will be too busy trying to keep their balance.

Rowing an inflatable against a headwind or tide is extremely difficult. In many rivers an adverse flow can be reduced or even avoided by rowing as close to the bank as practicable; however, there is seldom any satisfactory solution to a strong headwind. Very often youngsters like to practise rowing and a long light painter is an essential precaution at first. As their skills improve they can be allowed a closely defined area to row in and this must always be conducted upwind of the yacht, at or near slack water. Most parents, I'm sure, don't need to be reminded of the need for life-jackets and close supervision.

Now that the days of the cranky plywood 'pram' dinghy are over, a capsize is very rare due to the immense stability of most inflatable craft. However, turning at speed with an outboard going flat out is one way of giving everyone on board a wetting and, possibly, an unscheduled swim. Many of the bigger and more expensive inflatables now have a wooden stern piece (*transom*) and this makes them more stable as the air chambers extend beyond the engine. This prevents the dinghy capsizing in strong winds when moored alongside empty but with the engine in position. The ordinary type of inflatable tends to flip over when the wind gets under it. If you don't want to remove the engine the best solution is to secure the dinghy alongside with a short stern painter. I usually use the engine safety rope for this purpose.

3.14 ORDERS

Yet more jargon!

Helm orders	Meaning
Starboard/port your helm	Turn to right/left
Hard a starboard/port	Full lock
What's your heading?	State the present compass course
Bear away	Turn away from the wind
Luff/luff up	Turn towards the wind
Don't pinch	Increase the wind angle slightly (i.e. bear away)
Come ahead	Engage forward gear on engine
Go astern	Reverse
Half ahead/astern	Engine speed to 50%
Full ahead/astern	Maximum engine revs
Ease the wheel/helm	Decrease rudder angle

Cockpit orders	Meaning
Stand by to tack/gybe/come along-side	Prepare to tack/gybe/come along-side
Lee ho/helm a lee	Executive order to tack
Gybe ho	Executive order to gybe
Let go the sheet/halyard/warp	Release it completely
Ease the sheet/halyard/warp	Release it slowly under control
Free the sheet/halyard/warp	This request implies that the rope is tangled or jammed
Make fast	Twist rope round cleat/self-tailing winch, etc. Tie.

Foredeck orders	Meaning
Secure the sheet/halyard/warp	Similar to 'make fast'
Secure the anchor	This is a request to ensure that it is lashed down
Take a turn on the spring/headrope	Again similar to 'make fast' but implies that the rope in question is about to be under heavy load
Foul (as in 'foul anchor', 'foul sheet', etc.)	This is the nautical version of a snarl up
Hoist	Raise
Heave	Throw
Go aloft	Climb
Handsomely	Slowly (now rare)
Lively	Quickly (now rare)
Back	Reverse direction to the normal as in 'back water' (oars), 'back wind', etc.
Single up	Reduce to one only
All gone aft/forward	Not so much a command but a report that all mooring lines are off that section of the boat
Slip	Similar to 'let go'

Foredeck orders	**Meaning**
Round and back	Warp is led from the boat round a shore bollard and back on board and therefore easy to release

Reporting sightings	**Meaning**
Fine	Close to, as in 'fine on the port bow'
Abeam	Right angles
Abaft	Behind, as in 'abaft the beam' meaning more than 90° to the bow
Points	1/8 of a right angle: 4 points on the port bow indicates 45°.

4

TAKING AN INTEREST

4.1 NAVIGATION

Obviously no one is going to learn to navigate simply by reading a paragraph or two in a book such as this, although I must point out that navigation is nothing like as difficult as some people would have you believe. All we need to do here is to enable you to take an intelligent interest in what's happening on the chart table, especially when a passage is in the planning stage. Your main concern will probably be with the length of time the passage will take and to this end you need to know the distance involved.

As you may have gathered, nautical maps are known as *charts* and the universally accepted unit of distance both at sea and in the air is the *nautical mile* (symbol 'M'). The seaman's mile is about 12% longer than the land mile and is almost twice as long as the kilometre (1.854km = 1M). The great thing about 'M' is that it is equal to one minute of latitude. Now this fact may seem like an unnecessary complication to your life but it is vital. Only large-scale charts have one constant scale. On the great majority of charts you will search in vain for a scale or a statement about there being so many inches to the mile. Using a brass instrument that looks like a pair of school compasses (but with two points) called *dividers*, you first span the passage distance on the chart and then transfer to either the left or right margin but *never* to the top or bottom. (The latter are marked off in degrees and minutes of *longitude* and are not related to distance measurement.) On the east or west margins will be found the degrees and minutes of latitude. If your intended passage spans 1° then you are in for quite a trip of 60 nautical miles (60M). Remember one minute of latitude is 1 nautical mile and that like minutes in an hour, there are 60 minutes (written 60') to the degree.

Speed

Again the unit of speed at sea is universal and it is called the *knot* or nautical mile per hour. It follows that 8 knots is roughly 9 miles per hour or about 15km/hr.

Wind

If you have a forecast available put the dividers down on the chart to represent the wind direction. Judge the angle relative to your intended passage and you should begin to see what kind of wind angle you can expect. Generally speaking the bigger the angle the better and drier. Remember also to see if the wind is on or offshore. A fresh offshore wind can be good news, producing that dream of all sailors, plenty of wind but no sea.

4.2 TIDES

If you are sailing tidal waters the timing of your passage will be dominated by the direction of the water flow or *tidal stream*. Alternatively you may be unable to leave your present mooring until such time as the tide has risen. Again, tidal rhythms and tendencies are complex but a few basic guidelines will help. A typical month may start with tides that rise and fall (the *range*) only modestly; we call these *neaps*. A week later there will be a range of tide two or three times greater known as *springs*. After a further week we will be back on neaps (perhaps even smaller than those a fortnight ago). Finally, the cycle would finish with some energetic springs, perhaps four or five times greater than the tides a week previously.

The daily cycle in many parts of the world including most Atlantic coasts is for two tides a day (*diurnal*). This implies that *high* and *low water* are roughly every six hours; however, because this period is, on average, more rather than less than six hours, the period from high water to high water averages 12⅓ hours. This seemingly trivial difference results in the time of, say, high water advancing each day, typically by forty minutes.

Of all the mass of information one could give regarding tides I would pick one that should help to convey a useful picture, namely the importance of half tide, as the only fixed point in the system. Many newcomers to seafaring imagine that the tides move up from a lower fixed point (presumably low water) and simply rise higher on some days than others. The fact is that the same tide that rises to an exceptional height, i.e. a high water spring, also falls to an exceptionally low point. On neap tides both high and low levels are modest. The basic principle is that tides oscillate about a fixed point, namely half tide or *mean sea level*. This point is a constant for any particular port and only varies slightly with changes in barometric pressure.

A set of data for my own home port in Guernsey may be of help. Half tide or MSL for St Peter Port is fixed at 5m (16ft). An average spring tide rises to 9m (29ft) and falls to 1m (3ft), i.e. a spring range of 8m (26ft). Guernsey neap tides rise to just under 7m (23ft) and fall to just over 3m (9ft). 'From where,' might you ask, 'are the various levels measured?' Well, the answer is simply that an artificial level is used called *Chart Datum*. Chart Datum for most ports is now fixed at a level to which only the biggest and most exceptional spring tides ever fall. On charts this reference line is used downwards for depths (*soundings*) and upwards for the *drying height* of rocks and sandbanks provided that they cover at high water. Features that never cover are measured from a second reference line which is fixed at the level of an average high water spring.

4.3 WEATHER AND WEATHER FORECASTS

The weather is the one part of a cruise over which one has no control and all passage planning is dominated by it. At sea the concern is with wind and visibility; ashore most people are far more interested in rainfall and temperature. On most yachts, the main source of weather information is radio broadcasts, although fax machines and written bulletins play their part. The latter, perhaps posted up in the marina office, are often more easy to decipher than their spoken counterpart when cruising abroad.

One way to help the skipper or navigator to obtain weather information is to be aware of the times at which the shipping forecasts are broadcast and play your part in ensuring that they are not missed. This information should be available through the index of a nautical almanac. During the forecast peace and quiet are often essential as reception may be poor. The operation of electrical equipment, notably water pumps, can be disastrous. Mugging up on a few meteorological terms and their interpretation may prove useful.

Timing

Imminent	Within 6 hours
Soon	6 to 12 hours
Later	After 12 hours

Wind

Backing	Changing wind direction: moving anticlockwise
Veering	Opposite to backing
Moderating	Decrease in wind strength
Freshening	Increase in wind strength

Visibility

Fog	Less than 1,000 metres
Poor	1,000 metres to 2M
Moderate	2 to 5M
Good	5M plus
Fair	Used to describe the weather when there is nothing significant, i.e. no showers, mist or rain, etc.

Depression/low pressure/troughs	Bad news
Anticyclone/high pressure/ridges	Good news
Fronts (hot, cold and occluded)	Check your oilskins

Beaufort Wind Scale

Force	Wind speed in knots	Average wave height and sea condition	Effect on first time crew
0 calm	0–1 knot	Zero, mirror	Totally bored
1 light air	1–3 knots	Negligible, ripples	Bored
2 light breeze	4–6 knots	Wavelets	Less bored
3 gentle breeze	7–10 knots	1 foot, few white horses	Relaxed
4 moderate breeze	11–16 knots	3 feet, frequent white horses	Perfection
5 fresh breeze	17–21 knots	6 feet, many white horses	Demanding into wind
6 strong breeze	22–27 knots	10 feet, spray	Yachtsman's gale
7 near gale	27–33 knots	14 feet, foam streaks	Why did I come?
8 gale	34–40 knots	18 feet, spindrift	Terror threshold
9 severe gale	41–47 knots	23 feet, visibility reduced	Petrified (me too)
10 storm	48–55 knots	30 feet	Censored
11 violent storm	56–63 knots	36 feet	Censored
12 hurricane	64+	45 feet	Censored

4.4 INSTRUMENTS

Most of today's yachtsmen are great suckers for gadgetry, especially the electronic variety, and as a result there are usually a lot of dials, knobs and black boxes on most boats. Many are difficult for the novice to understand and it's best if you have them explained directly. However, be ready for the inevitable, 'Ah, yes, that one's not working,' or unbelievably, 'That one, yes, well that one's never worked,' etc.

Perhaps the most useful instrument to get to grips with is the *echo sounder* as there may be occasions when the helmsman wants the depths read out. There are two skills that need to be acquired; one is to do with the various scales and units. It could be disastrous for you to be happily calling the depths in fathoms when in fact they are in feet. The other skill is to master the running of the instrument – *adjusting the gain*, it is usually called. This can need frequent attention when echo sounding conditions are difficult. Generally speaking, rapidly changing readings require the gain to be reduced so as to find the true answer among all the false echoes. The gain is increased when the sounder fails to produce a reading or when it continually repeats the last accepted one.

As a total beginner you are likely to find Decca and radar, satellite navigators and autopilots complex beasts which are best left until your second or third cruise.

One rather good way of getting some free navigation instruction is to take the *bearings* for the navigator when a *visual position fix* is required and then watch as they are *plotted* on the chart. This entails using an instrument called a *hand bearing compass* and fortunately modern ones are easily mastered. Be wary of inducing seasickness when doing work of this nature as many an embryo navigator has succumbed to this particular peril.

If you are sailing with a very small crew then seek instruction, however basic, on the use of the boat's *VHF radio* transmitter. Although use of any transmitter is illegal until qualified this does not apply to an emergency situation.

4.5 RIGS

It would be nice, being the least experienced on board and probably regarded as a nautical nobody, to identify casually (and correctly) some obscure rig far away on the horizon, so here are a few tips:

- One mast and one headsail equals *sloop* (leave it to the pundits to decide if it is fractional or masthead)
- One mast and two or more headsails equals *cutter*.

Now there are three possibilities when dealing with two-masted vessels:

- Schooner – Big mast (main) nearer the stern.
- Ketch – Opposite to schooner.
- Yawl (now rare) – Like a ketch but with a tiny after-mast (mizzen) perched right on the stern.

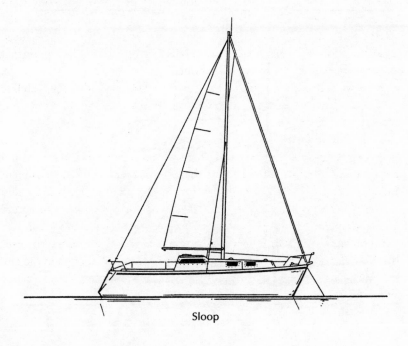

Sloop

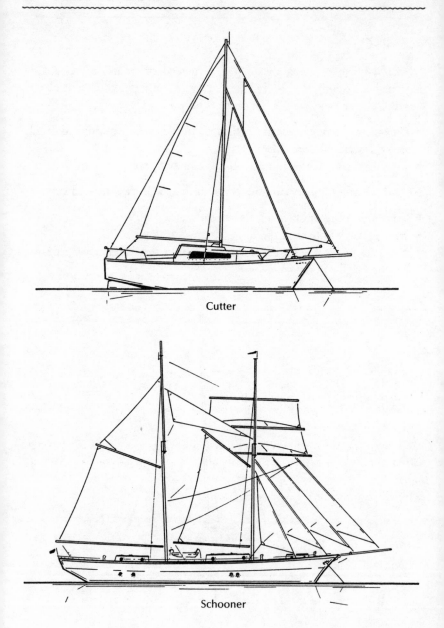

Cutter

Schooner

Ketch

Triangular mainsails signal *Bermudan rig*, but if on close examination the mainsail is seen to have four sides then the prefix is *gaff*. Thus we have 'gaff-rigged schooner' or 'Bermudan sloop'

Of course, there are many other possibilities but you now have ten rigs sorted out and they must account for 98% of the boats you are likely to sight.

Finally, whatever the rig – good sailing!